LIVING THE
VIVEKANANDA
WAY

Dr Ananya Awasthi is a public health expert and a passionate advocate for translating the timeless wisdom of Advaita Vedanta in ways that speak to today's youth. She is the Founder-Director of Anuvaad, a research and policy organization dedicated to strengthening India's health and nutrition systems through evidence-based insights. With a distinguished background in global health and public policy, Dr Awasthi previously led the India Research Center at the Harvard School of Public Health. A trained Hindustani classical vocalist, she holds a master's degree in public health from Harvard University. She regularly contributes writings and podcasts at the intersection of public health, well-being and Indic knowledge traditions.

Dr Nikhil Yadav is the author of अमृत काल में स्वामी विवेकानंद की प्रासंगिकता and *Influence of the Ramakrishna-Vivekananda Movement on Gandhi*. He currently serves as the Deputy Head of Vivekananda Kendra for the Uttar Prant region, overseeing activities in Delhi, Himachal Pradesh, Uttarakhand, and Jammu & Kashmir. A scholar of social sciences, Dr Yadav earned his PhD from the School of Social Sciences at Jawaharlal Nehru University (JNU). He also leads the youth outreach initiative 'Young India: Know Thyself', which has engaged over 1.5 lakh college students across the Delhi-NCR region in promoting a deeper awareness of Swami Vivekananda's message and its relevance for nation-building.

LIVING THE
VIVEKANANDA
WAY

PRACTICAL SPIRITUALITY
FOR MODERN INDIA

ANANYA AWASTHI
NIKHIL YADAV

Published by
Rupa Publications India Pvt. Ltd 2025
161-B/4, Gulmohar House,
Yusuf Sarai Community Centre,
New Delhi 110049

Sales centres:
Bengaluru Chennai
Hyderabad Kolkata Mumbai

Copyright © Ananya Awasthi and Nikhil Yadav 2025

The views and opinions expressed in this book are the authors' own and the facts are as reported by them; these have been verified to the extent possible, and the publishers are not in any way liable for the same.

All rights reserved.
No part of this publication may be reproduced, transmitted or stored in a retrieval system, in any form or by any means, electronic, mechanical, photocopying, recording or otherwise, without the prior permission of the publisher.

P-ISBN: 978-93-7003-341-2
E-ISBN: 978-93-7003-313-9

First impression 2025

10 9 8 7 6 5 4 3 2 1

The moral right of the authors has been asserted.

Printed in India

This book is sold subject to the condition that it shall not, by way of trade or otherwise, be lent, resold, hired out or otherwise circulated, without the publisher's prior consent, in any form of binding or cover other than that in which it is published.

Contents

Preface — *vii*

Introduction — *xi*

1. Life and Journey — 1
2. Taking Vedanta to the West — 20
3. Spiritual Teachings — 45
4. Impact on Modern-Day Leaders — 67
5. Relevance in the Contemporary World — 92
6. Call to Action for India's Youth — 115

Conclusion — 132

Annexure — 135

Glossary — 139

Bibliography — 145

Index — 151

Preface

In today's rapidly changing world, humanity is confronted with a host of pressing problems, ranging from issues of national security, interreligious strife and global developmental challenges to struggles over identity, survival and basic human rights. As societies grapple with these crises, there is a growing sense that conventional solutions are falling short. Increasingly, people are turning towards practical spirituality, seeking answers that transcend the boundaries of religion and offer meaningful guidance amid the chaos of modern life.

In an era marked by accelerated change, social unrest and personal disconnection, the question naturally arises: can ancient spiritual wisdom still offer meaningful guidance? More specifically, can spirituality truly be practical? Often, spirituality is equated with societal retreat—associated with monks, mountains and meditative solitude. It is commonly imagined as a choice between renunciation and material pursuit, leaving no middle ground. Swami Vivekananda shattered this false dichotomy. Through his life, teachings and heroic struggle, he redefined spirituality not as an escape from life but as its highest form of engagement—where the marketplace, classroom and home become grounds for inner growth and selfless service.

Spirituality has traditionally been closely linked with organized religion. However, in the modern era, particularly among the youth, there has been a notable return to timeless wisdom as a means of addressing complex contemporary problems. This book, inspired by the life and teachings of Swami Vivekananda, goes beyond a simple biography to explore the depth and relevance of his message.

Practical spirituality, as envisioned by Vivekananda, goes far beyond abstract theory or ritualistic observance. It is the realization of truth through lived experience, and its true measure lies in how it transforms thought into action. As the Swami succinctly put it, '[T]heory is very good indeed, but how are we to carry it into practice? If it be absolutely impracticable, no theory is of any value whatever, except as intellectual gymnastics. The Vedanta, therefore, as a religion must be intensely practical.' For him, Vedanta was not merely a system of ideas, but a living force meant to shape everyday life—challenging individuals to embody its ideals in the midst of work, struggle and service.[1]

In his *Raja Yoga* lectures, he presented a systematic method for spiritual realization, calling on seekers to explore the inner world with the same discipline that scientists apply to the external. Raja Yoga does not ask for blind faith; it demands a disciplined inquiry into the self, using the mind as the instrument of exploration. By focusing and refining the powers of concentration, seekers learn to penetrate the layers of the inner world and realize the deeper currents that shape life itself. Vivekananda's message was profoundly

---

[1] Swami Vivekananda, 'Practical Vedanta: Part I', *The Complete Works of Swami Vivekananda Vol. II*, Advaita Ashrama, Uttarakhand, 2016, p. 285.

empowering: the external world is but a reflection of the inner world, and by mastering the internal forces, one can shape destiny. In an age of restless questioning and deep inner hunger, Vivekananda's call resounds with even greater urgency—that spirituality must not remain locked in distant scriptures or inherited dogmas but must become a living, luminous force, realized in the hearts of those who dare to seek and to experience it for themselves.[2]

At its core, this book highlights how Vivekananda's teachings have practical applications in day-to-day life. Vivekananda's vision is anchored in the non-dualistic philosophy of Advaita, which acknowledges the fundamental unity of existence. The philosophy espouses that although people may differ in colour, religious affiliation or geographical location, they are all part of the same universal consciousness. Rooted in the spiritual oneness of humanity, his teachings offer a template for finding common solutions to the shared challenges facing our world. Although the narrative is grounded in the Indian context, his teachings provide a framework for individuals and communities across the globe to address contemporary issues from a place of spiritual clarity.

This is what makes Vivekananda's message timeless. He taught that true freedom comes not through wealth or power but through mastery over the self—through detachment, clarity, compassion and unwavering service. He called upon individuals to seek the 'divine' not in distant heavens but within themselves and among their fellow beings.

---

[2]Swami Vivekananda, 'Introductory', *The Complete Works of Swami Vivekananda Vol. I*, Advaita Ashrama, Uttarakhand, 2016, pp. 123–34.

For Vivekananda, serving the poor and the oppressed was the highest form of worship. His was a call to awaken the sleeping soul of humanity—to discover strength within and then direct it outwards for the good of all. In doing so, he offered a model of how the highest ideals can shape everyday life, reform society as well as political vision.

In this spirit, we invite readers to engage with the ideas presented here, not merely as a reflection on the past but as a guide for living in the present. By embracing the principles of spiritual oneness and practical action, we believe that Swami Vivekananda's teachings have the potential to inspire a brighter, more inclusive future for all.

Introduction

Swami Vivekananda emerged at a time when India was in need of a voice that could unite its timeless spiritual wisdom with the aspirations of a new era. His vision was to inspire a renaissance of thought and action grounded in India's profound heritage, yet fully engaged with the modern world. He sought not only to revive the country's spiritual and cultural identity but also to awaken the masses—particularly the youth—with a sense of pride, purpose and patriotism. Carrying the essence of India's ancient scriptures beyond its shores, Vivekananda presented the true spirit of his motherland to the West, establishing Vedanta Societies in countries like the United States of America (USA) and England and gathering a devoted circle of admirers and disciples around him, including Sister Nivedita and J.J. Goodwin. Whether in Madras (now Chennai), Lahore (now in Pakistan), or his birthplace, Calcutta (now Kolkata), his message remained consistent: to break free from the shackles of British oppression through education, organization and national awakening.

In 1897, Vivekananda established the Ramakrishna Mission to carry forward the ideals of his *guru* (teacher/mentor), Sri Ramakrishna Paramhansa. It was one of the first organized attempts in the country to blend Vedantic spiritual practice with dedicated service to humanity. His vision extended beyond religious revival. Recognizing the need for scientific and intellectual advancement, he inspired the creation of institutions like the Indian Institute of Science in Bangalore (now Bengaluru), embodying the seamless integration of ancient wisdom with modern inquiry. At the same time, he fiercely criticized the divisions, jealousy and inertia that he believed were eroding the nation's strength, urging Indians to cultivate unity, self-confidence and fearless action.

In the brief but intense period between his return to India and his *mahasamadhi*[1] in 1902, Vivekananda laid the groundwork for a transformative movement—ranging from the founding of journals like *Prabuddha Bharata* and *Udbodhan* to the establishment of educational institutions such as the girls' school in Calcutta founded by Sister Nivedita and schools in Alwar, Khetri and Udaipur started by Swami Akhandananda. In Madras, Swami Ramakrishnananda set up a branch of the Ramakrishna Mission, extending Vivekananda's vision to the south. During the plague epidemic in Calcutta—in the last decade of the twentieth century—extensive community service was carried out under his guidance, demonstrating his emphasis on practical compassion. Beyond these efforts, hundreds of initiatives inspired by his life and teachings took root across the country, affirming the enduring impact of his mission to awaken, serve and unite humanity.[2]

---

[1] On 4 July 1902, Swamiji took *mahasamadhi*—the conscious and intentional departure from the body by a *yogi*, regarded as the ultimate liberation.
[2] *The Life of Swami Vivekananda by His Eastern and Western Disciples Vol.*

One of Vivekananda's most enduring contributions was his articulation of the Vedanta's essence—a doctrine that reveals the fundamental unity of all life and humanity—in a modern, universal language. At a time when India was grappling with profound existential questions about the meaning of its civilizational heritage and how to reconcile its spiritual traditions with the forces of modernity, Vivekananda emerged as a beacon of clarity and renewal. With a spirit both revolutionary and fearless, he redefined the understanding of 'God', 'worship' and 'service', urging a break from ritualistic compliance and the adoption of an active, living spirituality. His stirring call to recognize the *virat*—the divine in our fellow beings—marked a seismic shift in India's spiritual and national consciousness. In his monumental lecture delivered more than a century ago, Vivekananda proclaimed that the highest form of worship should be dedicated to serving and uplifting the people of India, for it is within them that 'God' is truly awake. Rather than chasing after distant ideals, he emphasized that honouring the virat—the collective and universal form manifest in humanity—was the first and most urgent duty.[3]

Reflections from eminent thinkers underline the magnitude of Vivekananda's contribution. Sarvepalli Radhakrishnan, the second president of India and one of the country's foremost academicians, offered a deeply insightful perspective on Vivekananda's significance. He observed: 'The city of Calcutta has produced many men of genius

---

II, Advaita Ashrama, Uttarakhand, 1989, pp. 430–38.
[3]Swami Vivekananda, 'The Future of India', *The Complete Works of Swami Vivekananda Vol. III*, Advaita Ashrama, Uttarakhand, 2016, p. 315.

in education, science, literature and spiritual endeavour, and one of the greatest of them all is Swami Vivekananda. He embodied the spirit of this country. He was a symbol of her spiritual aspirations and fulfilment.' Radhakrishnan recognized in Vivekananda not merely a religious figure but the very articulation of India's eternal soul—the voice of its sages, the devotion of its people and the wisdom of its ancient philosophies. He urged that remembering the Swami is not enough; it is essential 'to understand what he wished us to do,' to 'assimilate his teachings, incorporate them in our being,' and strive to be worthy citizens of the nation that produced such a spirit. In reflecting on Vivekananda's contributions, Radhakrishnan's words remind us that his relevance lies not only in the past but also in the continuous shaping of India's moral and spiritual destiny.[4]

The French Nobel laureate Romain Rolland reflected that though Vivekananda's call to awaken the soul of India was electrifying, people's immediate response to it was limited. Rolland poignantly asked, 'Did the dead arise? Did India, thrilling to the sound of his words, reply to the hope of her herald? Was her noisy enthusiasm translated into deeds?'[5] Even as Vivekananda himself expressed disappointment at the hesitant emergence of the dynamic youth he had envisioned, Rolland noted that the true significance of Vivekananda's message lay deeper: like a 'rough scourge,' it roused the ancient, slumbering soul of India, planting within

---

[4]Majumdar, R.C. (ed.), *Swami Vivekananda Centenary Memorial Volume*, Swami Vivekananda Centenary, Calcutta, 1963, p. xiii.
[5]Swami Vivekananda, *My India: The India Eternal* [1st ed.], Ramakrishna Mission Institute of Culture, Kolkata, 2019, pp. 214–17.

it the seeds of a profound and irreversible awakening—one whose full flowering would take decades but whose first movement had already begun.

Vivekananda's thunderous appeal—likened to a storm scattering fire and water across the land—would later blossom into the Bengal revolt, Tilak's agitation, Gandhi's mass movements and the collective action of a once-dreaming nation. Rolland recognized that the Swami's message carried both a national and universal meaning: while rooted in Advaita's universal spirit, it was the national call that revived India's strength. He saw modern India's leaders—such as Aurobindo, Tagore and Gandhi—as fruits of the 'double constellation' of Ramakrishna's soul and Vivekananda's heroic action. Thus, Rolland credits Vivekananda as the herald who began the true forward march of India, a march whose echoes still shape her destiny.[6]

For those seeking to understand Vivekananda's life, philosophy and influence more deeply, several notable works stand out. *The Complete Works of Swami Vivekananda*, a nine-volume series, obviously offers the most authentic and comprehensive account of his teachings, philosophy and vision. To complement this, Sister Nivedita's *The Master as I Saw Him* stands as a remarkable work, offering rare personal insights into his life and character. Sister Gargi's *Swami Vivekananda in the West: New Discoveries*, a six-volume series, is another outstanding resource that provides a detailed and complementary perspective on his time and influence in the West. *Rousing Call to Hindu Nation* by

---

[6]Rolland, Romain, *The Life of Vivekananda and the Universal Gospel*, Advaita Ashram, Uttarakhand 2018, p. 239.

Eknath Ranade was one of the first successful attempts to compile Swami Vivekananda's essential messages into a concise and accessible form.

Among biographies, *Vivekananda: A Biography* by Swami Nikhilananda is an ideal choice for new readers, providing a clear and engaging introduction. For a more detailed account, *The Life of Swami Vivekananda by His Eastern and Western Disciples*, in two volumes, offers valuable reflections and anecdotes from those who knew him personally. Additionally, *A Comprehensive Biography of Swami Vivekananda* by Sailendra Nath Dhar, spanning three volumes, presents an even deeper and more exhaustive account. For Western audiences, Romain Rolland's *The Life of Vivekananda and the Universal Gospel* remains a highly recommended read.

Building upon this understanding of Vivekananda's life, teachings and vision, the chapters that follow take a deeper look into the various dimensions of his extraordinary impact. Each chapter is designed to offer a focused exploration, from tracing his personal journey and spiritual awakening to unpacking his powerful teachings, examining his influence on modern leaders and assessing his continued relevance in today's world. Through these explorations, the book seeks to present not just a portrait of a remarkable individual but a timeless guide for anyone seeking purpose, strength and unity in an ever-evolving world.

In the first chapter, we delve into the life and journey of Vivekananda, a man whose simplicity and depth of purpose set him apart. Though he never claimed to be an incarnation of God, his actions were so profound that many regarded him as a spiritual figure of great significance. From his early life in a wealthy family to the hardships he faced after his father's death, Vivekananda's quest for answers to life's most fundamental and existential questions remained unwavering. His transformative encounter with Sri Ramakrishna at the Dakshineshwar Temple profoundly reshaped his spiritual journey, ultimately answering the most profound question: 'Have you seen God?' Vivekananda's travels across the country acted as spiritual explorations that solidified his unique form of nationalism, deeply rooted in the essence of India.

The second chapter looks into Vivekananda's journey to the West where he propagated the essence of Vedanta—the universal message of oneness and brotherhood. His remarkable appearance at the World Parliament of Religions, held in Chicago, USA, catapulted him onto the global stage, introducing the West to the profound wisdom of ancient Indian traditions. His Western disciples, inspired by his teachings, furthered his work, dedicating themselves to India. On his return, Swami Vivekananda initiated numerous projects aimed at helping India recover from centuries of foreign rule and regain her strength.

The third chapter focuses on the influential teachings of the Swami that are becoming more relevant with each passing day. His words, often described as electric shocks, emanated from his deep conviction in—and a comprehensive understanding of—ancient Indian scriptures. Vivekananda presented these teachings with a scientific temperament, making them accessible and effective for addressing the challenges of contemporary society. His message of self-confidence, unity and spiritual empowerment continues to resonate with individuals and communities worldwide.

In the fourth chapter, we examine the impact of Vivekananda on Indian leaders in both the pre- and post-Independence eras. His life and message left a lasting impression on countless influential figures across various fields. Although it is nearly impossible to measure the full extent of his influence, this chapter offers a tribute to the profound effect Vivekananda had on shaping the thoughts and actions of Indian leaders. Renowned Indologist A.L. Basham emphasized the challenge of fully evaluating Vivekananda's importance in world history. He suggested that Vivekananda's impact was far more profound than acknowledged by his contemporaries, stating that in centuries to come, he will be remembered as one of the key figures who shaped the modern world.[7]

The fifth chapter evaluates the contemporary relevance of Vivekananda, particularly focusing on how his teachings can guide today's youth. We identify some of the key challenges that young people face in today's world—such as identity, mental health and the search for purpose—and offer solutions drawn from his teachings. His timeless wisdom and visionary insights provide a roadmap for navigating these challenges and empowering the youth to move forward with confidence and clarity.

Finally, in the sixth chapter, we discuss the call to action that Vivekananda extended to the youth. He emphasized the responsibility each individual holds in building a

---

[7] Swami Ghanananda and Geoffrey Parrinder (eds.), *Swami Vivekananda in East and West*, Ramakrishna Vedanta Centre, London, 1968, pp. 210–14.

stronger nation and how understanding and implementing his message can lead to a life of purpose and fulfilment. His words continue to inspire today's generation to rise to the challenge, embrace their potential and contribute meaningfully to society.

This book, through its exploration of Vivekananda's life, teachings and enduring impact, seeks to highlight how his wisdom offers meaningful answers to the complex challenges of our times. In a world divided by conflict, inequality and cultural tensions, Vivekananda's call to recognize the 'divine' in every being and to build a society grounded in compassion, courage and unity is timeless. His profound teaching—service to others is the highest form of worship—continues to inspire a path of action that uplifts the marginalized and reaffirms the dignity of all life. For the youth navigating ambition and uncertainty, his message of inner strength and fearless self-belief offers a clear and empowering guide. Above all, the Swami's vision bridges ancient Indian spiritual wisdom with the needs of a modern, interconnected world, offering a blueprint for national renewal and universal brotherhood. This book invites readers to not only rediscover the ideals that shaped India's awakening but also embody them—pursuing personal growth anchored in service, unity and a deep sense of spiritual oneness.

1

Life and Journey

The Socio-Political-Cultural Milieu

The story of Swami Vivekananda's life and journey cannot be fully understood without first appreciating the world he inherited. The British presence in India, which began in the late sixteenth century with exploratory missions by merchants, quickly evolved from a trading relationship into political domination. The establishment of the first English factory in Surat in 1612 marked the beginning of formal relations. However, it was the decisive victories at the battles of Plassey (1757) and Buxar (1764) that cemented British political control over vast territories within India. By the early nineteenth century, the British East India Company had not only consolidated economic power but also begun reshaping Indian society and culture. Thomas Babington Macaulay's document 'Minute on Education' (1835) aimed to produce a class of Indians who were 'Indian in blood and colour, but English in taste, in opinions, in morals, and in intellect,' further eroding indigenous traditions.[1]

The uprising of 1857, India's first war of independence, though ultimately suppressed, marked a pivotal shift. The East India Company was dissolved and India came under direct rule of the crown, initiating the era of the British Raj. During Vivekananda's lifetime (1863–1902), India bore the deep scars of colonial policies: systematic economic exploitation, cultural denigration, widespread famines and a profound crisis of identity. Indian traditions were increasingly portrayed as inferior and a deep cultural dissonance divided the Western-educated elite from their heritage.

Yet, this period also witnessed stirrings of renewal. Bengal, especially Calcutta, the intellectual and political heart of British India, became a centre of socio-religious reform movements such as the Brahmo Samaj. Reformers sought to eradicate superstition, caste discrimination and social injustices while reviving the ethical essence of Indian spirituality. Alongside these reformist efforts, revivalist currents reasserted the dignity of India's ancient culture. Amid this churn of decay and regeneration, a deep yearning for national pride and self-assertion was taking root.

It was into these turbulent, conflicted times that Vivekananda was born. His emergence was not just timely—it was transformative. Recognizing that India's regeneration could not come from mere imitation of the West nor from blindly clinging to the past, Vivekananda offered a dynamic vision: a revival of India's spiritual traditions interpreted

---

[1]Macaulay, T.B., 'Macaulay's Minute on Education', Central Secretariat Library, Government of India 1835, p. 9, https://tinyurl.com/yj65fvfu. Accessed on 2 May 2025.

through the lens of rational inquiry, fearless action and national service. Growing up in Calcutta, Vivekananda absorbed the intellectual ferment of his time even as he rooted himself in the timeless wisdom of Vedanta.

Meeting his guru, Sri Ramakrishna Paramhansa, became the defining moment of his life. Sri Ramakrishna taught him to see God in every living being—a realization that fuelled Vivekananda's mission to combine spiritual realization with the active service of humanity. His travels across India, encountering the lives, sufferings and aspirations of its people, deepened his conviction that India had an enduring spiritual message to offer the world and that the revival of national pride must be grounded in both cultural self-respect and practical service.

When he rose to speak at the World Parliament of Religions in Chicago, 1893, the world heard not just an individual but the voice of a resurgent India. His speeches captured the global imagination with Vedanta's universal message of oneness and brotherhood. Upon returning to India, the Swami galvanized the youth with a call to awaken out of centuries of stagnation and dedicate themselves to the task of national regeneration. From Colombo to Lahore, he travelled tirelessly, sowing seeds of strength, pride and service wherever he went.

In a nation burdened by colonial rule and fractured by internal divisions, Vivekananda emerged as a beacon of hope, self-belief and spiritual resurgence. His life was a clarion call to India—and humanity at large—to experience true freedom through the realization of one's inner divinity and the service of mankind. This chapter traces the inspiring journey of Vivekananda, exploring how a fearless monk awakened a slumbering nation and offered a timeless vision that continues to inspire the world even today.

Birth, Childhood and Family

Swami Vivekananda was born in Calcutta on 12 January 1863, coinciding with the auspicious day of Makar Sankranti. He was the sixth of 10 children born to Bhuvaneshwari Devi and Vishwanath Datta. Professionally a well-established lawyer, Vishwanath Datta was also a creative person with a passion for music. Datta lived in a joint family at 3 Gour Mohan Mukherjee Street in Calcutta. Bhuvaneshwari Devi, while traditional at heart, was a strong-willed patriot who instilled cultural values and a spirit of service in her children from a very early age.

Vivekananda had an active and vibrant childhood. A restless young boy, he was full of energy and had a large circle of friends. He enjoyed a range of activities, including wrestling, swimming and cooking, and even built a gymnasium in his courtyard with his friends.[2] Moreover, his father had created a 'zoological garden' within their home premises. This garden housed a variety of pets and birds. He especially adored the family cows and maintained his passion for animals and birds until his last day in Belur Math.

At age six, Vivekananda attended primary school for the first time. While he was still lovingly called 'Biley' at home, he was registered as 'Narendranath' in the school.

---

[2]Dhar, Sailendra Nath, *A Comprehensive Biography of Swami Vivekananda Vol. 1*, Vivekananda Kendra Prakashan Trust, Chennai, 2012, p. 43.

The young boy had an early introduction to meditation. As a child, he would sit in a meditating posture before idols of Hindu deities. He later recounted these experiences in his lectures and discourses.[3]

Early introduction to Bengali and Sanskrit helped Narendranath in his lifelong study of ancient manuscripts. At school, he was passionate about subjects such as Sanskrit, English and history, but not mathematics. He also actively engaged in various activities that promoted holistic development and drew him closer to spiritual life; for instance, Narendranath would lead a celebration of 'Vandemata' where students from the school marched down the banks of Ganga with flags, music and chants, eulogizing the holy river as a mother.[4]

When he was in his ninth grade, he was transferred to an institution founded by Pandit Ishwar Chandra Vidyasagar. Thereafter, in 1877, his father got transferred to Raipur (in present-day Chhattisgarh). Since Raipur did not have a formal school, Narendra was home-schooled by his father for a couple of years.

College Days

In 1879, the family returned to Calcutta, and Narendranath continued his education there. After completing school,

---

[3] Swami Vivekananda, 'The Powers of the Mind', *The Complete Works of Swami Vivekananda Vol. II,* Advaita Ashrama, Uttarakhand, 2016, pp. 21–22

[4] Dhar, Sailendra Nath, *A Comprehensive Biography of Swami Vivekananda Vol. 1*, Vivekananda Kendra Prakashan Trust, Chennai, 2012, pp. 55–56.

he enrolled in Presidency College—one of Calcutta's most prominent colleges—having cleared its entrance examination in the first division. However, in his very first year, he contracted malaria and suffered from extreme bouts of fever, which largely disrupted his studies. He was unable to attend even the minimum number of lectures required to appear for the examination. Consequently, the college establishment refused to let him continue, and he had no choice but to take a transfer to the Scottish Church College. In 1881, he passed the First Arts Examination[5] with a second division. This was also the year he met his guru, Sri Ramakrishna Paramhansa, at the Dakshineswar Kali Temple, located to the north of Calcutta. Three years later, Narendranath finished his bachelor's degree from the same college.

From playing sports to learning music or regularly spending time at the banks of the holy Ganga, Narendranath, like any other young boy of his age, had a diverse set of experiences. He had a thriving friend circle and was a member of the Brahmo Samaj.

He passionately read both Indian and Western literature throughout his undergraduate years. He did not limit himself to his textbooks and perceived the university examinations as just a medium to earn credentials. He studied a wide range of texts, including but not limited to Green's *History of the English People*, Alison's *History of Europe*, and Gibbon's *The Decline and Fall of the Roman Empire*, in addition to curriculum textbooks like Elphinstone's *The History of India*, Marshman's *Outline of the History of Bengal*, Jevons's

---

[5]Ibid., p. 66.

Elementary Lessons in Logic and *Studies in Deductive Logic*.

Narendranath had a deep interest in history, whether it was ancient India or the French Revolution. Swami Saradananda's accounts suggest that Vivekananda also read a diverse range of works by Western philosophers, including Descartes, Hume, Kant, Fichte, Spinoza, Hegel, Schopenhauer, Comte, Darwin, Mill, Locke and Plato. The philosophy of Herbert Spencer captivated his interest the most. At the same time, Narendranath started examining Hinduism through the lens of logical reasoning. This inclination to prioritize reason over imagination or blind faith becomes more apparent in the subsequent trajectory of his life. His brilliance and intellect were recognized by the principal of Scottish Church College, Mr William Hastie. He observed, 'Narendra Nath Dutta is really a genius. I have travelled far and wide but have never yet come across a lad of his talent and possibilities, even in German universities, amongst philosophy students.'[6]

Interestingly, equipped with a sharp memory and the keen ability to grasp new and complex concepts, he developed a unique method of reading and learning. Vivekananda describes this peculiar habit in his own words:

> It so happened that I could understand an author without reading his book line by line. I could get the meaning by just reading the first and the last line of the paragraph. As this power developed, I found it unnecessary to read the paragraphs. I could follow by

---

[6]Dhar, Sailendra Nath, *A Comprehensive Biography of Swami Vivekananda Vol. 1*, Vivekananda Kendra Prakashan Trust, Chennai, 2012, pp. 68–69.

reading only the first and the last lines of a page. Further, where the author introduced discussions to explain a matter and it took him four, or five, or even more pages to clear the subject, I could grasp the whole trend of his arguments only by reading the first few lines.[7]

In February 1884, tragedy struck when his father, Vishwanath Datta, died of a heart attack. Narendranath was all of 21 when he experienced this emotional setback. It was a confusing time in his life. He had recently started visiting the high court, working as an assistant to Nimai Charan Bose, his father's friend and a well-known lawyer. At the same time, marriage proposals had begun coming his way. The grief of his father's demise added to the burgeoning uncertainty the young man was already facing regarding his life's mission and purpose.

Vishwanath Datta's death led to his family facing a lot of socio-economic adversities. Describing the challenging times, Vivekananda (1889) wrote of his mother and siblings, 'They were quite well off before, but since my father's death, it is going very hard with them—they even have to go fasting at times! To crown all, some relatives, taking advantage of their helplessness, drove them away from the ancestral residence.'[8]

---

[7]Ibid., p. 69.
[8]Swami Vivekananda, 'Epistles-Second Series—VII', *The Complete Works of Swami Vivekananda Vol. 6*, Advaita Ashrama, Uttarakhand, 2016, p. 220.

Meeting Ramakrishna Paramhansa

Sri Ramakrishna Paramhansa was born as Gadadhar Chattopadhyay in 1836 in Kamarpukur village in the Hooghly district of Bengal Presidency (present-day West Bengal). With no formal schooling, he came to Dakshineswar and became a priest in a temple dedicated to Kali Thakur. Here he did 12 years of *sadhana* or spiritual training under Sri Tota Puri, a Vedantist. Tota Puri gave him the name 'Ramakrishna'—a fully realized soul capable of achieving *nirvikalpa samadhi* in a single day. Ramakrishna later married Saradamani Mukhopadhyay, who came to be known as Sarada Devi. He regarded Sarada Devi as his spiritual companion and an incarnation of the divine mother who helped him in his spiritual journey. Ramakrishna's disciples addressed her as the 'Holy Mother'.

There is no definitive, reliable information on how Narendranath first learnt about Ramakrishna. Some speculate that he heard of him through the Brahmo Samaj, while others claim that he learnt about Ramakrishna from his teacher William Hastie. Reportedly, while describing the poem 'The Excursion' by William Wordsworth, Hastie suggested that if his students wanted to meet a person in a state of trance, they should visit Ramakrishna Paramhansa in Dakshineswar. Still others believe that Narendranath first met his guru at the residence of his neighbour, Surendranath Mitra, who had requested that he sing some *bhajan*s (hymns) in his home during Ramakrishna's stay. Moved by his singing, Ramakrishna invited him to

Dakshineswar.[9] However, another account from *The Gospel of Sri Ramakrishna* points out that it was Narendranath's relative, Sri Ramchandra Datta, a chemist by training, who brought him to Ramakrishna.[10]

On 15 January 1882, Narendranath—accompanied by Surendranath Mitra, Ramchandra Datta and his friends—visited the saint. Ramakrishna asked him to sing some songs. Thereafter, he took the latter's hand and led him into an empty room, where he began weeping with joy. He exclaimed, 'Ah, you come so late! My ears are well-nigh burnt in listening to the profane talks of the worldly people.'[11]

Another significant event occurred the same day and served as a turning point in Narendranath's life. During his meeting with Ramakrishna, he received an answer to the question that had haunted him for years: 'Has anyone seen God?' He had been relentlessly seeking an answer to this question and had placed it before various notable figures, including Devendranath Tagore who was associated with the Brahmo Samaj. Vivekananda narrated this conversation between himself and Ramakrishna in one of his lectures, titled 'My Master':[12]

---

[9]Dhar, Sailendra Nath, *A Comprehensive Biography of Swami Vivekananda Vol. 1*, Vivekananda Kendra Prakashan Trust, Chennai, 2012, pp. 105–09.

[10]*The Gospel of Sri Ramakrishna* (Red Letter Edition) was originally recorded in Bengali by M., a disciple of Sri Ramakrishna; Sri Ramakrishna Math Mylapore, Chennai, 1942, (Red Letter Ed. 2000), p. 48.

[11]Dhar, Sailendra Nath, *A Comprehensive Biography of Swami Vivekananda Vol. 1*, Vivekananda Kendra Prakashan Trust, Chennai, 2012, p. 118.

[12]Ibid., pp. 119–20.

> I heard of this man, and I went to hear him. He looked just like an ordinary man, with nothing remarkable about him. He used the simplest language, and I thought can this man be a great teacher?— crept near to him and asked him the question which I had been asking others all my life: Do you believe in God, Sir? "Yes," he replied. Can you prove it, Sir? "Yes." How? "Because I see Him just as I see you here, only in a much intenser sense." That impressed me at once. For the first time I found a man who dared to say that he saw God, that religion was a reality to be felt, to be sensed in an infinitely more intense way than we can sense the world. I began to go to that man, day after day, and I actually saw that religion could be given. One touch, one glance, can change a whole life.[13]

The seed of a new movement was thus sown. It would sweep the country—with Calcutta as its epicentre—and influence millions of people in the decades to come.

Legacy of Ramakrishna Paramhansa

Ramakrishna's wisdom illuminated Narendranath's life, helping him finally find answers to the questions he had been grappling with. He now looked to Ramakrishna as his guru, literally 'one who takes a person out of darkness.' But he was not a blind believer. With an analytical approach, he examined and tested Ramakrishna for over five years to

---

[13]Swami Vivekanada, 'My Master', *The Complete Works of Swami Vivekananda Vol. IV*, Advaita Ashrama, Uttarakhand, 2016, p. 174.

eliminate his doubts and questions. His devotion towards his guru can be understood from these words: '[I]f I have told you one word for truth, it was his [Ramakrishna's] and his alone, and if I have told you many things which were not true, which were not correct, which were not beneficial to the human race, they were all mine, and on me is the responsibility.'[14]

This *guru-shishya* (teacher-student) relation or *shraddha* (devotion) is deeply meaningful in its strength, purity and selflessness. As Vivekananda observed, 'The more such men are produced in a country, the more that country will be raised; and that country where such men absolutely do not exist is simply doomed, nothing can save it.'[15] Indeed, in some sense, it would be fair to say that Swami Vivekananda would not exist without the enduring influence of Sri Ramakrishna Paramhansa.

> **Romain Rolland on Ramakrishna**
>
> In his biography of Ramakrishna, titled *The Life of Ramakrishna*, the French Nobel laureate Romain Rolland wrote, 'The man whose image I here evoke was the consummation of two thousand years of the spiritual life of three hundred million people. Although he has been dead forty years, his soul animates modern India. He was no hero of action like Gandhiji, no genius in art or thought like Gandhiji or Tagore. He was a little village Brahmin of Bengal whose outer life was set in a limited frame without

---

[14] Ibid., p. 181.
[15] Ibid., p. 182.

> striking incident, outside the social and political activity of the time. But his inner life embraced the whole multiplicity of men and Gods.'[16]

'Purity' was the defining quality of Vivekananda's character since childhood. He possessed an overwhelming zeal for righteousness in all areas of life, extending beyond merely resisting what is wrong. Based on the Vedanta philosophy, he concluded that spiritual existence is impossible without purity. When his involvement in spiritual pursuits exposed him to the life of a *sanyasi* (monk; one who drifts in the direction of God's will, uncertain of where he may get his meals or the opportunity to rest, with the open sky being the only constant in his life), Vivekananda had the option of choosing between a conventional life—marriage, family, children, worldly gains—and the austere life of a monk, and he selected the latter. He chose *tyag* (renunciation) and *seva* (service) and never looked back.[17]

A Spiritual Journey through India

After Ramakrishna attained *samadhi* in 1886, Narendranath was given the organizational duty to keep his *gurubhai*s (spiritual brothers following the same guru) together.

---

[16]Rolland, Romain, *The Life of Ramakrishna*, Advaita Ashrama, Uttarakhand, 2023, p. XXII.
[17]Swami Vivekananda, *Collegiate Days—Tendencies*, https://www.swamivivekananda.guru/2017/12/23/collegiate-days-tendencies/. Accessed on 15 July 2025.

He gathered the young disciples of Ramakrishna and decided to begin a spiritual training by converting a dilapidated house in Baranagar into a *math* (monastery). The days spent at Baranagar Math marked the beginning of a new chapter, with Narendranath emerging as the guiding force. All the 16 monastic disciples of Ramakrishna changed their names as they began their journey into monkhood. Narendranath took upon the monastic name 'Vividishananda'.

Having left his home, name and identity to answer Ramakrishna's call to serve the motherland, Vivekananda was now prepared to become a *parivrajaka sanyasi* (wandering monk). In 1888, he left the Baranagar Math with only a *kamandalu* (water pot) and a copy of the Srimad Bhagavad Gita in his hand to explore the country and spread his message.[18] Over the next five years, he travelled widely around India, learning about its people and culture. He visited various towns, including Ayodhya, Lucknow, Agra, Vrindavan, Hathras, Ghazipur, Prayag, Nainital, Almora, Srinagar, Dehradun, Rishikesh and Haridwar in present-day Uttar Pradesh and Uttarakhand. Almora remained one of the Swami's favourite places which he visited several times with his gurubhais and Western disciples. It was also the place where he delivered one of his first public lectures in Hindi during his welcome reception after the successful campaign in the West.[19]

---

[18]Before embarking on his nationwide journey, Swami Vivekananda made two unsuccessful attempts to leave Belur Math. His first journey was interrupted by ill health and the second journey by the sudden demise of his close associates Balram Babu and Suresh Chandra Mitra.

[19]Swami Vivekananda, 'Address of Welcome at Almora and Reply',

Vivekananda also travelled through Meerut and Delhi before turning to Rajasthan and visiting Alwar, Jaipur, Ajmer, Mount Abu and Khetri, where he met Maharaja Ajit Singh. Thereafter, he travelled to Gujarat, stopping in Ahmedabad, Wadhwan, Limbdi, Girnar, Kutch, Porbandar, Dwaraka, Palitana, Nadiad, Baroda and Kathiawar.

Vivekananda's stay in Porbandar, situated in the western part of the Kathiawar peninsula, was particularly significant. It was here that he completed his study of Panini's grammar and also met Pandit Shankar Pandurang, *dewan* (administrator) of Porbandar and a learned Sanskrit scholar. Pandurang was a well-travelled man with extensive knowledge of foreign languages and a big library which attracted Vivekananda's attention. Pandurang is quoted to have said, 'Swamiji, I am afraid you cannot do much in this country. Few will appreciate you here. You ought to go to the West where people will understand you and your worth. Surely you can throw a great light upon Western culture by preaching the Sanatana Dharma!' This aligned with what Swami had already been thinking. Moreover, wherever he travelled and in every court that he visited, the princes and pandits alike perceived in him that same 'terrible restlessness' to do something meaningful for his country.[20]

According to various accounts, it was in Porbandar or Junagarh (in Kathiawar) that Vivekananda first learned of a major religious convention to be held the following

---

The Complete Works of Swami Vivekananda Vol. III, Advaita Ashrama, Uttarakhand, 2016, p. 364.

[20]*The Life of Swami Vivekananda by His Eastern and Western Disciples Vol. 1*, Advaita Ashrama, Uttarakhand, 1989, pp. 295–96

year in Chicago. When the idea of travelling to the West and attending the Parliament of Religions first took shape in his mind, his primary intention was to share India's spiritual wisdom with the world and, following Pandit Pandurang's advice, to explore a synthesis between Eastern and Western thought. The notion of raising funds for his countrymen—later mentioned by some writers—does not appear to have been a significant motive for the Swami at that initial stage.[21]

Thereafter, he travelled to Mahabaleshwar in Maharashtra and Indore and Khandwa in Madhya Pradesh. He also visited Margao and Panaji in Goa, and Belgaum and Bangalore in Karnataka. His journey continued with stops in Thrissur, Kodungalloor, Trivandrum and Ernakulam in Kerala. Thereafter, he set off on foot for Tamil Nadu, visiting Nagercoil and Kanyakumari, where he found his life's mission at the southernmost tip of the country. After Kanyakumari, he visited Madras, Pondicherry, Madurai and Rameswaram.

Throughout his journey, Vivekananda relied on *bhiksha* (alms) and commuted primarily on foot, and on occasion by train when his devotees provided the ticket. He stayed with kings and dewans as well as with the poorest of the poor. His travels across India were, in fact, more than physical journeys; they were deep encounters with the soul of the nation, an exploration of its spiritual vitality, its struggles and its potential for renewal.

He learnt a profound lesson in the sacred city of Varanasi

---

[21]Dhar, Sailendra Nath, *A Comprehensive Biography of Swami Vivekananda Vol. 1*, Vivekananda Kendra Prakashan Trust, Chennai, 2012, p. 442.

that would later become emblematic of his teachings—courage in the face of adversity. Recalling an incident there, he narrated, 'The monkeys of Varanasi are huge brutes... As they pressed closer, I began to run, but the faster I ran, the faster came the monkeys... Just then I met a stranger who called out to me, "Face the brutes." I turned and faced the monkeys, and they fell back and finally fled.' This, he said, was a life lesson—face challenges boldly and they retreat.[22] In Ayodhya, the birthplace of Lord Rama, whom he had adored since childhood, Vivekananda immersed himself in the spirit of the Ramayana, reconstructing in his mind the sacred scenes of a divine past. His pilgrimage took him to Vrindavan next, where he walked the last 30 miles on foot to reach the land of Krishna.[23]

In Rajasthan, encounters with disciples led to discussions about not just philosophical truths but also the practical realities of Indian society. To a disciple lamenting the incompatibility of truthfulness and modern economic life, Vivekananda offered a vision rooted in India's ancient traditions. He advocated for the revitalization of agriculture through scientific methods, stating, 'If educated men go to live in the villages [...] if agriculture is carried on scientifically, then the yield will be more.' Through such efforts, he believed, the divide between castes could be bridged, and the true education of the masses could be achieved.[24]

---

[22] Swami Vivekananda, 'What Is Religion', *The Complete Works of Swami Vivekananda Vol. I*, Advaita Ashrama, Uttarakhand, 2016, p. 328.
[23] *The Life of Swami Vivekananda by His Eastern and Western Disciples Vol. 1*, Advaita Ashrama, Uttarakhand, 1989, p. 217.
[24] Ibid., pp. 273–75.

His journey southward brought him to Bombay (now Mumbai), where he met Lokmanya Bal Gangadhar Tilak, who later recounted how the simply dressed young sanyasi—carrying only a deerskin, a few cloths and a kamandalu—captivated everyone around him. At the Deccan Club in Poona, Vivekananda impressed the gathering with his lucid exposition of the Advaita philosophy, speaking extemporaneously in flawless English. Tilak remembered, 'Everyone there was thus convinced of his high abilities.' Yet, true to his monastic spirit, Vivekananda soon left silently, seeking no fame or recognition. Whether in casual conversations about village upliftment or in philosophical debates about Vedanta, Vivekananda's deep love for the people and profound commitment to India's spiritual awakening were constant. His journeys thus laid the foundation for his later triumph at the World Parliament of Religions in Chicago, where he would bring the essence of India's timeless wisdom to the global stage.[25]

Meditation at Kanyakumari

After travelling across the length and breadth of the country, Vivekananda reached Kanyakumari, the southernmost tip, in December 1892. He meditated on a rock, approximately 500 metres off the mainland of India, for three days and nights (25, 26 and 27). During his meditation, Vivekananda analysed the causes of India's demise and the means of its resurrection.

---

[25]Ibid., pp. 306–07.

> In a letter—dated 19 March 1894—to his gurubhai Ramakrishnananda from Chicago, Vivekananda wrote, 'My brother, in view of all this, specially of the poverty and ignorance, I had no sleep. At Cape Comorin sitting in Mother Kumâri's temple, sitting on the last bit of Indian rock—I hit upon a plan […] That those poor people are leading the life of brutes is simply due to ignorance […] We, as a nation, have lost our individuality, and that is the cause of all mischief in India. We have to give back to the nation its lost individuality and *raise the masses*.'[26]

---

[26]Swami Vivekananda, 'Epistles-Second Series— XLI Shashi', *The Complete Works of Swami Vivekananda Vol. VI*, Advaita Ashrama, Uttarakhand, 2016, p. 266.

2

Taking Vedanta to the West

While meditating in Kanyakumari, Swami Vivekananda reflected deeply on the 'regeneration of the Motherland' and spreading the message of Vedanta to the West.[27] With deep introspection into the reasons behind the country's abysmal state and the means of its resurrection, the Swami took the historic decision to travel to the West. The main obstacle in the way of realizing this vision was the lack of necessary funds to support his journey to the United States (US) to attend the World Parliament of Religions. Vivekananda's young disciples, led by Maharaja Alasinga Perumal of Mysore, Maharaja Ajit Singh of Khetri and the Raja of Ramnad, all came together to lend their support for this historic voyage.[28]

From the works of Romain Rolland, we learn that before departing for Chicago to participate in the Parliament of Religions, the Swami changed his name to 'Vivekananda' at

---

[27]Dhar, Sailendra Nath, *A Comprehensive Biography of Swami Vivekananda Vol. 1*, Vivekananda Kendra Prakashan Trust, Chennai, 2012, pp. 524–25.
[28]Swami Vivekananda, *Chicago Addresses*, Advaita Ashrama, Uttarakhand, 2018, pp. 9–11.

the suggestion of Maharaja Ajit Singh. Until then, he had been known by several names, including 'Vividishananda' and 'Satchidananda'. The name 'Vivekananda' would soon become famous worldwide after the speech delivered at the World Parliament.[29]

Vivekananda's lectures in the West—the famous series delivered in Chicago at the World Parliament of Religions, academic discourse at Harvard University, interactions with figures like Max Müller and John D. Rockefeller, and the establishment of Vedanta Societies across America—laid the groundwork for a deeper East–West dialogue on philosophy, psychology and religion. *Raja Yoga*, his seminal work composed in the United States, translated ancient yogic thought into a language accessible to the modern mind and forever changed how spirituality was understood in the West. But his influence didn't end there. This global recognition reverberated back home, rejuvenating a sense of national pride and identity among Indians. The Vedanta, that once lay dormant under the weight of colonial rule, now emerged as the philosophical backbone of India's renaissance. Thus, Vivekananda's mission marked not only the advent of Vedanta in the modern West, but also its revitalization in India—a bridge of thought and spirit that continues to inspire across generations and geographies.

Early Hardships

On 31 May 1893, Swami Vivekananda left India to attend the

---

[29]Rolland, Romain, *The Life of Vivekananda and the Universal Gospel*, Advaita Ashram, Uttarakhand, 2018, p. 5.

World Parliament of Religions. Travelling through China, Japan and Canada, he reached Chicago at the end of July 1893. However, upon reaching the United States, the Swami discovered that the Parliament of Religions would not begin until September and only delegates nominated from an institution were permitted to participate. Furthermore, the deadline for delegate admission and registration had passed.

Vivekananda's early experiences in the US were marked by profound hardships that tested his resilience and inner strength. Arriving in a foreign land with little money, he struggled to adapt to the unfamiliar environment. The approaching winter was particularly harsh; even in August, New England's climate was extremely cold for him and without adequate warm clothing, he faced severe physical discomfort. Financial strain also weighed heavily on him—the necessary winter clothing alone cost nearly a hundred dollars, a significant sum that left little for living expenses.[30]

His traditional Hindu dress made him a conspicuous figure; he was often jeered at in the streets and even physically harassed. At the Chicago World's Fair, a man disrespectfully pulled at his turban, only to recoil in embarrassment when Vivekananda calmly addressed him in English. On another occasion, after being pushed from behind, Vivekananda confronted his assailant, who stammered, 'Why do you dress that way?' In Boston, he narrowly escaped a mob that pursued him with jeering remarks and threats.[31]

---

[30] *The Life of Swami Vivekananda by His Eastern and Western Disciples Vol. 1*, Advaita Ashrama, Uttarakhand, 1989, p. 404.
[31] Dhar, Sailendra Nath, *A Comprehensive Biography of Swami Vivekananda Vol. 2*, Vivekananda Kendra Prakashan Trust, Chennai, 2012, pp. 566–67.

Despite these repeated indignities and assaults, Swami Vivekananda's spirit remained unshaken. Although the idea of returning to India crossed his mind in moments of difficulty, he firmly resolved to exhaust every effort in the US before considering retreat, and if needed, to try his luck in England. His determination was rooted in a deeper conviction—that no great mission could be accomplished without sacrifice and suffering. Fully aware that he was facing not just a cultural gap but also prejudice and ignorance, he bore these hardships with patience and dignity, seeing them as necessary trials on the path to fulfilling his greater purpose. His quiet perseverance amid adversity revealed the immense strength of his character: a mind unshaken by ridicule, a heart sustained by faith and a will forged through hardship—ready to share India's timeless wisdom with a sceptical world.

In a lecture delivered in San Francisco (18 March 1900), Vivekananda declared, 'Even in your country where you think you are highly educated, how full of narrowness and superstitions you are! Just think, with all your claims to civilisation in this country, on one occasion I was refused a chair to sit on, because I was a Hindu.'[32]

---

[32]Swami Vivekananda, 'Buddha's Message to the World', *The Complete Works of Swami Vivekananda Vol. VIII*, Advaita Ashrama, Uttarakhand, 2016, pp. 98–99.

> **Meeting Professor Wright**
>
> Vivekananda recalled meeting with Ms Kate Sanborn on a train journey from Vancouver. In her autobiography *Abandoning An Adopted Farm*, Ms Sanborn wrote:
>
>> But most of all I was impressed by the monk, a magnificent specimen of manhood-six feet two, as handsome as Salvini (a then famous Italian actor) at his best, with a lordly, imposing stride, as if he ruled the universe, and soft, dark eyes that could flash fire if roused, or dance with merriment if the conversation amused him...
>>
>> He wore a bright yellow turban many yards in length, a red ochre robe, the badge of his calling; this was tied with a pink sash, broad and heavily befringed. Snuff-brown trousers and russet shoes completed the outfit. He spoke better English than I did, was conversant with ancient and modern literature, would quote easily and naturally from Shakespeare or Longfellow or Tennyson, Darwin, Muller, Tyndall; could repeat pages of our Bible, was familiar with and tolerant of all creeds. He was an education, an illumination, a revelation!
>>
>> I told him, as we separated, I should be most pleased to present him to some men and women of learning and general culture, if by any chance he should come to Boston.[33]

---

[33] Sanborn, Kate, *Abandoning An Adopted Farm,* D. Appleton and Company, New York. 1906, pp. 7-10.

> Impressed by Vivekananda's mission, Sanborn invited him to stay over at her village home in Massachusetts, near Boston. Vivekananda graciously accepted her invitation. Through her, he met several prominent personalities, including Kate's cousin Franklin Benjamin Sanborn (an author, journalist and philanthropist) and Mr John Henry Wright, a professor of Greek at Harvard University.[34] Professor Wright was so impressed with Swami Vivekananda that he recommended that he speak at the World Parliament of Religions. When Swami Vivekananda informed him that he lacked the required credentials, Professor Wright responded, 'To ask you, Swami, for credentials is like asking the sun to state its right to shine.' Professor Wright wrote a letter of recommendation to the chairman of the Parliament, suggesting that Swami Vivekananda be invited as a speaker. 'Here is a man who is more learned than all our learned professors put together.'[35] [36]

The World Parliament of Religions

Despite facing severe challenges, Vivekananda reached the World Parliament of Religions with a message for the world. In a letter from Chicago to his disciple Alasinga Perumal, he shared his experience of delivering the famous speech on

---

[34] *The Life of Swami Vivekananda by His Eastern and Western Disciples Vol. I*, Advaita Ashrama, Uttarakhand, 1989, pp. 403–04.

[35] Bhuyan, P.R., *Swami Vivekananda: Messiah of Resurgent India*, Atlantic Publishers & Dist, New Delhi, 2003, p. 16.

[36] Bhide, Nivedita Raghunath, *Swami Vivekananda in America*, Vivekananda Kendra Prakashan Trust, Chennai, 2002, p. 15.

11 September 1893. He described the grand procession, the sight of a hall and gallery packed with six to seven thousand attendees, representing the cultures of their countries, alongside learned men from around the world on the platform. Despite never having spoken in front of the Western public before, the Swami faced this distinguished audience.

He admitted to feeling extremely nervous—his heart was racing and his tongue was nearly dry—causing him to refrain from speaking in the morning session. With no speech prepared, he reposed his trust in Devi Saraswati and stepped up when introduced by Dr Barrows. He began his address with 'Sisters and Brothers of America', which received a deafening, two-minute applause. By the end of his sermon, he was exhausted with emotion.

The next day, newspapers hailed his speech as the highlight of the event, making him known throughout the US.

Original Transcript of the Welcome Address Delivered by Swami Vivekananda

Sisters and Brothers of America,

It fills my heart with joy unspeakable to rise in response to the warm and cordial welcome which you have given us. I thank you in the name of the most ancient order of monks in the world; I thank you in the name of the mother of religions; and I thank you in the name of millions and millions of Hindu people of all classes and sects.

My thanks, also, to some of the speakers on this

platform who, referring to the delegates from the Orient, have told you that these men from far-off nations may well claim the honour of bearing to different lands the idea of toleration. I am proud to belong to a religion which has taught the world both tolerance and universal acceptance. We believe not only in universal toleration, but we accept all religions as true. I am proud to belong to a nation which has sheltered the persecuted and the refugees of all religions and all nations of the earth. I am proud to tell you that we have gathered in our bosom the purest remnant of the Israelites, who came to Southern India and took refuge with us in the very year in which their holy temple was shattered to pieces by Roman tyranny. I am proud to belong to the religion which has sheltered and is still fostering the remnant of the grand Zoroastrian nation. I will quote to you, brethren, a few lines from a hymn which I remember to have repeated from my earliest boyhood, which is every day repeated by millions of human beings: "*As the different streams having their sources in different places all mingle their water in the sea, so, O Lord, the different paths which men take through different tendencies, various though they appear, crooked or straight, all lead to Thee.*"

The present convention, which is one of the most august assemblies ever held, is in itself a vindication, a declaration to the world of the wonderful doctrine preached in the Gita: "*Whosoever comes to Me, through whatsoever form, I reach him; all men are struggling through paths which in the end lead to me.*" Sectarianism, bigotry, and its

> horrible descendant, fanaticism, have long possessed this beautiful earth. They have filled the earth with violence, drenched it often and often with human blood, destroyed civilisation and sent whole nations to despair. Had it not been for these horrible demons, human society would be far more advanced than it is now. But their time comes; and I fervently hope that the bell that tolled this morning in honour of this convention may be the death-knell of all fanaticism, of all persecutions with the sword or with the pen, and of all uncharitable feelings between persons wending their way to the same goal.[37]

Swami Vivekananda delivered six speeches during the 17-day Parliament of Religions (11–27 September 1893). He also gave some lectures in the Parliament's scientific section, the script for which is unavailable.[38]

Speeches Delivered by Swami Vivekananda at the World Parliament of Religions

Date	Topic of the Speech
11 September 1893	'Response to Welcome'
15 September 1893	'Why We Disagree'
19 September 1893	'Paper on Hinduism'

---

[37] Swami Vivekananda, 'Response to Welcome', *The Complete Works of Swami Vivekananda Vol. I*, Advaita Ashrama, Uttarakhand, 2016, pp. 3–4.
[38] Dhar, Sailendra Nath, *A Comprehensive Biography of Swami Vivekananda Vol. 2*, Vivekananda Kendra Prakashan Trust, Chennai, 2012, pp. 630–37.

20 September 1893	'Religion Not the Crying Need of India'
26 September 1893	'Buddhism, the Fulfilment of Hinduism'
27 September 1893	'Address at the Final Session'

Swami Vivekananda also delivered several lectures at Harvard University. On 25 March 1896, he spoke about 'The Vedanta Philosophy'[39] at the Graduate Philosophical Society of Harvard University.[40] Thereafter, he was asked to join Harvard University—an offer he declined.[41] Romain Rolland notes that alongside the Chair of Oriental Philosophy at Harvard, Vivekananda was also offered the Chair of Sanskrit at Columbia University.[42] One of Vivekananda's lectures was covered by *The Harvard Crimson*, the university's student newspaper, which found his address 'interesting' and 'impressive' and praised his 'clear and eloquent voice'.[43]

---

[39]Swami Vivekananda, 'The Vedanta Philosophy', *The Complete Works of Swami Vivekananda Vol. I*, Advaita Ashrama, Uttarakhand, 2016, pp. 347–55.
[40] Swami Vivekananda, 'Discussion at The Graduate Philosophical Society of Harvard University', *The Complete Works of Swami Vivekananda Vol. V*, Advaita Ashrama, Uttarakhand, 2016, p. 303.
[41]Gupta, Raj Kumar, *The Great Encounter: A Study of Indo-American Literary and Cultural Relations*, Abhinav Publications, New Delhi, 1986, p. 118.
[42]Rolland, Romain, *The Life of Vivekananda and the Universal Gospel*, Advaita Ashrama, Uttarakhand, 2018, p. 67.
[43]*The Harvard Crimson*, 'Vivekananda's Address', 17 May 1894, https://tinyurl.com/2k9583ku. Accessed on 2 May 2025.

Raja Yoga: Swami Vivekananda's Masterpiece

While travelling through the West, Vivekananda came up with a book titled *Raja Yoga*. The book draws from his comprehension and analysis of Patanjali's *Yoga Sutras*. Written on Western soil, his commentaries were crafted with a Western audience in mind. Vivekananda details Rishi Patanjali's Ashtanga Yoga (the eight limbs) in his work. He writes, 'Râja-Yoga is divided into eight steps. The first is Yama—non-killing, truthfulness, non-stealing, continence, and non-receiving of any gifts. Next is Niyama—cleanliness, contentment, austerity, study, and self-surrender to God. Then comes Âsana, or posture; Prânâyâma, or control of Prâna; Pratyâhâra, or restraint of the senses from their objects; Dhâranâ, or fixing the mind on a spot; Dhyâna, or meditation; and Samâdhi, or super consciousness.'[44]

According to the Swami, concentration is essential for gaining knowledge; without it, nothing significant can be accomplished. Ordinary individuals waste most of their mental energy, leading to frequent mistakes, whereas the trained mind avoids errors. By focusing inward, one can master their inner faculties rather than being dominated by them. While the Greeks achieved external excellence in art and literature through concentration, Hindus focused on the inner self, developing yoga, which teaches control over the senses, will and mind. This practice allows us to become masters of ourselves instead of being controlled by external forces. Swami Vivekananda wrote, 'Yoga is controlling the

---

[44]Swami Vivekananda, *Raja Yoga: Conquering the Internal Nature*, Advaita Ashrama, Uttarakhand, 2023, p. 33.

senses, will, and mind. The benefit of its study is that we learn to control instead of being controlled.'[45]

Influencing the Western Mind

On 9 July 1895, Vivekananda wrote a letter to Maharaja Ajit Singh from the US, saying, 'I have planted a seed in this country; it is already a plant, and I expect it to be a tree very soon. I have got a few hundred followers. I shall make several Sannyâsins, and then I go to India leaving the work to them.'[46] The 'seed' Swami Vivekananda is most likely referring to is the 'Vedanta Society of New York', which he established in November 1894. When Vivekananda left for India, he called upon his gurubhai, Swami Abhedananda, to take care of the society.

Romain Rolland

One of the finest works on Vivekananda in pre-Independent India is by Romain Rolland. *The Life of Vivekananda and the Universal Gospel*, published in 1931, offers a vivid and compelling portrayal of Vivekananda's life and teachings. Though it is primarily intended for Western readers, it is an excellent resource for all admirers of the Ramakrishna movement.

According to Rolland, Vivekananda's success in Chicago was not merely an individual achievement but a national

---

[45]Swami Vivekananda, 'Concentration', *The Complete Works of Swami Vivekananda Vol. VI*, Advaita Ashrama, Uttarakhand, 2016, p. 133.
[46]Swami Vivekananda, 'Epistles-First Series—XLVIII', *The Complete Works of Swami Vivekananda Vol. V*, Advaita Ashrama, Uttarakhand, 2016, p. 87.

victory and a source of pride for the entire country.[47] He beautifully describes his work: 'Under the dry and brilliant sky of New York with its electric atmosphere, Vivekananda's genius for action burned like a torch and consumed him in the midst of a world of frenzied activity. His expenditure of power in thought, writing, and impassioned speech dangerously compromised his health.'[48]

John D. Rockefeller

The encounter between Vivekananda and John Davison Rockefeller is both significant and intriguing. During his first visit to the West, Vivekananda stayed in the Chicago home of a business associate of John D. Rockefeller who repeatedly encouraged him to meet the Swami.

Accepting his invitation, Rockefeller paid Vivekananda an unexpected visit and found him in his room, deeply engrossed in his writing. He was so absorbed in his work that he did not even glance up to acknowledge Rockefeller's presence.[49] After sometime, 'Vivekananda told Rockefeller much of his past that was not known to any but himself, and made him understand that the money he had already accumulated was not his, that he was only a channel and that his duty was to do good to the world—that God had given him all his wealth in order that he might have an opportunity

---

[47]Rolland, Romain, *The Life of Vivekananda and the Universal Gospel*, Advaita Ashram, Uttarakhand, 2018, p. 85.
[48]Ibid., p. 70.
[49]Swami Vivekananda, 'Conversations and Interviews', *The Complete Works of Swami Vivekananda Vol. IX*, Advaita Ashrama, Uttarakhand, 2016, pp. 352–53.

to help and do good to people.'[50] Indifferent to Swami's advice, Rockefeller went away without saying anything.

He returned a week later and slammed a paper on the table. It detailed his plans to donate a huge amount of money to an organization. He said to Vivekananda, 'You must be satisfied now, and you can thank me for it.'[51] The Swami took the paper without raising his head and read it slowly, before calmly stating, 'It is for you to thank me.'[52] Rockefeller had never made such a sizable donation before; it was his first such contribution to society at large.[53]

Josiah Goodwin

To preserve the literary treasure and wisdom of Swami Vivekananda, his disciples in the West decided to document his lectures. An advertisement was published in *The Herald* and *The World* on 12 December 1895 in New York to hire a shorthand writer.[54] Goodwin, who was 25 years old at the time, was selected for the position, and in no time, he transformed from an employee to a devoted disciple. In a conversation with one of the gurubhais of Vivekananda, Goodwin said, 'I have been to many places, mixed with many people, then in America I met Swami Vivekananda. Then alone I could understand what love was. So, income or no income, I am trapped! I have been rounding the world,

---

[50]Ibid.
[51]Ibid.
[52]Ibid.
[53]Ibid.
[54]Pravrajika Vrajaprana, *My Faithful Goodwin*, Advaita Ashrama, Uttarakhand, 2015, pp. 4–5.

hobnobbed with famous people, but never have I found such a noble being as Swami Vivekananda: one is drawn as if to one's very own.'[55]

Goodwin continually documented almost all of Vivekananda's lectures for over a year. He was nothing less than a shadow of Vivekananda. He received *brahmacharya* (celibacy) vows from Vivekananda, who also wanted to train him as a Vedanta teacher. His devotion towards Vivekananda can be understood from the letter that he wrote to Josephine MacLeod[56] on 7 October 1896: 'Shall I shock you very much if I tell you that the Swami takes the place of Christ to me? I think not, for you will understand what I mean.'[57]

When Vivekananda decided to return to India at the end of 1896, he asked Goodwin to accompany him. Goodwin agreed. Despite being an Englishman, he never demonstrated any colonial or racial superiority. This interpersonal dynamic is exemplified by an instance where he did not hesitate from washing Vivekananda's feet as a disciple in front of an Indian crowd.[58] He travelled with

---

[55]Ibid., p. 10.
[56]Josephine MacLeod was an American devotee of Swami Vivekananda who worked tirelessly in promoting the Vedanta and Ramakrishna movement in the West and India. She was only five years older than Swamiji and deeply devoted to him and his work. (Pravrajika Atmaprana, *Western Women in the Footsteps of Swami Vivekannada*, Ramakrishna Sarada Mission, Hauz Khas, New Delhi, 1995, pp. 99–100.) Swamiji often addressed her endearingly as 'Dear Joe Joe' in his letters. (Swami Vivekananda, 'Epistles-Fourth Series—LIV', *The Complete Works of Swami Vivekananda Vol. VIII*, Advaita Ashrama, Uttarakhand, 2016, p. 341.)
[57]Ibid., p. 33.
[58]Ibid., pp. 86–87.

Vivekananda from Madras to Lahore. Unfortunately, his health deteriorated due to the change in climate and environment, and he fell seriously ill, passing away at just 27 years of age. Vivekananda was in Almora when he got this news. Grief-stricken, he declared, 'Now my right hand is gone. My loss is incalculable.'[59]

Professor Max Müller

Vivekananda felt deeply honoured by an invitation from Professor Max Müller to visit his home in Oxford. During their meeting, they engaged in profound discussions on Indian philosophy, with a particular focus on Ramakrishna. Vivekananda recounted this meeting in an article for the magazine *Brahmâvadin* on 6 June 1896.[60] He expressed profound admiration for Müller and viewed the visit as a pilgrimage due to the professor's deep respect for Ramakrishna.

Müller was inspired to write about Ramakrishna after observing significant changes in Keshub Chandra Sen, who had been influenced by the saint. He enquired about the efforts being made to promote Ramakrishna's teachings and offered to write a comprehensive account if provided with sufficient material. Vivekananda promptly requested Swami Ramakrishnananda to gather and send the necessary documents to him. This collaboration led to Müller's book *The Life and Sayings of Sri Ramakrishna* and his article in

---

[59]Ibid., p. 104.
[60]Swami Vivekananda, 'On Professor Max Müller', *The Complete Works of Swami Vivekananda Vol. IV*, Advaita Ashrama, Uttarakhand, 2016, pp. 270–75.

The Nineteenth Century magazine, which significantly aided Vivekananda's efforts in England to generate interest in Ramakrishna's teachings.[61]

Although Müller occasionally criticized certain aspects of Hinduism, Vivekananda continued to hold him in high personal regard. His efforts in popularizing Ramakrishna and supporting the Vedanta movement were invaluable.[62]

∞

During his three-and-half-year stay in the West (May 1893 to January 1897), Vivekananda introduced and propagated Indian Vedantic thought to Western audiences. He travelled to several parts of the US and England, as well as countries such as Switzerland, Germany and France. Vivekananda's impact was so profound that thousands of people attended his lectures, and some were influenced to such a great extent that they followed him back to India to offer their services; Christina Greenstidel, who later became Sister Christine, Capt. Sevier and his wife Charlotte Sevier, and the aforementioned J.J. Goodwin were a few of them. Sister Christine—recollecting Vivekananda's classes in the US—said, 'Millionaires were glad to sit on the floor, literally at his feet.'[63] And it was during his visit to England that Sister

---

[61] Max Müller published an article called 'A Real Mahatman' in the August 1896 issue of *The Nineteenth Century* magazine, which was a British monthly periodical established in 1877 by Sir James Knowles.

[62] Dhar, Sailendra Nath, *A Comprehensive Biography of Swami Vivekananda Vol. 2*, Vivekananda Kendra Prakashan Trust, Chennai, 2012, pp. 1095–1105.

[63] Ibid., pp. 975–76.

Nivedita got inspired by Swami Vivekananda's vision and was called upon to work for women's education in India.

Mentoring Social and Spiritual Work in India from the West

Vivekananda, while sharing spiritual wisdom with the West, continued to mentor spiritually oriented social work in India. Some glimpses of this mentorship can be seen in the letters he wrote to his gurubhais and disciples in India while he was abroad. In a letter to his gurubhai Swami Akhandananda, he wrote:

> Go from door to door amongst the poor and lower classes of the town of Khetri and teach them religion. Also, let them have oral lessons on geography and other subjects. No good will come of sitting idle and having princely dishes, and saying "Ramakrishna, O Lord!"—unless you can do some good to the poor. Go to other villages from time to time and teach the people the arts of life as well as religion. Work, worship, and Jnana (knowledge)—first work, and your mind will be purified; otherwise, everything will be fruitless like pouring oblations on a pile of ashes instead of in the sacred fire. [...] [M]ove from door to door of the poor and the destitute in every village of Rajputana. [...] The Geruâ robe is not for enjoyment. It is the banner of heroic work. You must give your body, mind, and speech to "the welfare of the world". You have read—मातृदेवोभव, पितृदेवोभ—"Look upon your mother as God, look upon your father as God"—but I say दरिद्रदेवोभव,

मूर्खदेवोभ—The poor, the illiterate, the ignorant, the afflicted—let these be your God. Know that service to these alone is the highest religion.[64]

Return to India

After returning to India in January 1897, Vivekananda dedicated his time and energy to the task of national regeneration by covering the length and breadth of the land—from Rameshwaram to Rawalpindi, Kashmir to Kanyakumari and Dehradun to Dhaka. For the next two-and-a-half years (January 1897 to June 1899), he delivered lectures throughout the country, giving electrifying speeches that were meant to be a roadmap for India's future. Some of the most important among them were 'My Plan of Campaign', 'The Sages of India', 'The Work before Us', 'The Future of India', 'The Common Bases of Hinduism' and 'The Vedanta'. These lectures were attended by large gatherings, particularly the youth. He was welcomed, celebrated and even worshipped in several places as a God.[65]

Vivekananda spoke about himself in detail for the first time at Victoria Hall in Madras, while delivering the 'My Plan of Campaign' lecture in 1897. He shared some of his experiences over the preceding 14 years, essentially since his father's death in 1884:

---

[64]Swami Vivekananda, 'Epistles-Second Series—LV', *The Complete Works of Swami Vivekananda Vol. VI*, Advaita Ashrama, Uttarakhand, 2016, p. 298.
[65]Pravrajika Vrajaprana, *My Faithful Goodwin*, Advaita Ashrama, Uttarakhand, 2015, pp. 79–81.

A man who has met starvation face to face for fourteen years of his life, who has not known where he will get a meal the next day and where to sleep, cannot be intimidated so easily. A man, almost without clothes, who dared to live where the thermometer registered thirty degrees below zero, without knowing where the next meal was to come from, cannot be so easily intimidated in India. This is the first thing I will tell them—I have a little will of my own. I have my little experience too; and I have a message for the world which I will deliver without fear and without care for the future.[66]

Such was his courage and conviction for the task of awakening the nation. Nothing could deter him; not even the fear of death.

> **Founding of the Ramakrishna Mission**
>
> On 1 May 1897, Swami Vivekananda founded the Ramakrishna Mission (RKM), named after Sri Ramakrishna Paramhansa. The mission was set up to provide organizational and systematic support to the Ramakrishna movement. Inspired by the virtues of renunciation and service, the monks and the followers of the mission believe in perceiving a living God in the people they serve. Through medical, educational and spiritual service, the mission continues to impact millions across the globe.[67]

---

[66] Swami Vivekananda, 'My Plan of Campaign', *The Complete Works of Swami Vivekananda Vol. III*, Advaita Ashrama, Uttarakhand, 2016, pp. 227–28.
[67] *Belur Math*, 'Branch Centres', https://tinyurl.com/37mvpwdu. Accessed on 29 March 2022.

Second Visit to the West

Despite his failing health, Vivekananda travelled to the West for a second time in June 1899. He was accompanied by Sister Nivedita and his gurubhai Swami Turiyananda.[68] Sister Nivedita regarded this trip with the Swami as 'the greatest occasion' of her life.[69] On 31 July 1899, Swami Vivekananda landed in London, where he met some of his disciples and visited Sister Nivedita's home in Wimbledon. Upon meeting him, Mary and Richmond, Sister Nivedita's two younger siblings, also became dedicated to Vivekananda and his cause. With Swami Turiyananda and a couple of his American disciples, Swami Vivekananda left for the US in August 1899. He delivered a few lectures in New York and in cities across California—Los Angeles, Pasadena and San Francisco—before moving on to Paris, where he participated in the Congress of the History of Religions. While there, he also attended the International Congress of Physics, alongside the renowned scientist Jagadish Chandra Bose.[70]

After returning to India in December of 1900, he visited the Advaita Ashramas in Mayavati (now in Uttarakhand), Dhaka and Chandranath (both in present-day Bangladesh). He also travelled to Kamakhya in Assam, Shillong (present-day Meghalaya), Bodhgaya in Bihar and Varanasi in Uttar Pradesh. Rest of his time was spent at the Belur Math in

---

[68]Dhar, Sailendra Nath, *A Comprehensive Biography of Swami Vivekananda Vol. 3*, Vivekananda Kendra Prakashan Trust, Chennai, 2012, p. 1607.
[69]Ibid., p. 1606.
[70]Ibid., pp. 1756–57.

the company of his gurubhais and young *brahmachari*s.[71] Despite his failing health, he continued to work tirelessly for his mission. According to him, '[O]ur bodies have to go; there is no permanence about them. Blessed are they whose bodies get destroyed in the service of others.'[72]

The Master as I Saw Him

Vivekananda was deeply concerned about women's education in India and he called upon his Irish disciple, Margaret Elizabeth Noble (Sister Nivedita), to take this work forward. In her book titled *The Master as I Saw Him,* Sister Nivedita recalled that during a conversation 'he turned to me and said, "I have plans for the women of my own country in which you, I think, could be of great help to me."'[73] She further wrote that 'I knew that I had heard a call which would change my life.'[74]

Inspired by the Swami's speeches in the West, Margaret Noble left her homeland and arrived in India on 28 January 1898, where the Swami personally welcomed her.[75] She adapted swiftly to Indian conditions, and Swami Vivekananda guided her through the Indian knowledge system. Sister Nivedita established a girls' school on Bosepara Lane,

---

[71]Ibid., p. 1774.
[72]Swami Vivekananda, 'Universal Love and How it Leads to Self-Surrender', *The Complete Works of Swami Vivekananda Vol. III*, Advaita Ashrama, Uttarakhand, 2016, p. 94.
[73]*Nivedita of India,* Ramakrishna Mission Institute of Culture, Kolkata, 2016, p. 28.
[74]Ibid.
[75]Ibid., pp. 3–4.

Calcutta, despite a severe lack of resources. She inaugurated the first school on 13 November 1898, which was also blessed by Sri Sarada Maa. In the days that followed, she enrolled local women and widows and began their education.[76]

Sister Nivedita recorded her personal experiences, significant events and information about Vivekananda and the people around him in her book. Her writings give us a close account of Vivekananda's life and mission, as exemplified in the statement, 'The thought of India was to him like the air he breathed.'[77] The three major influences on his life were his education in English and Sanskrit; Guru Sri Ramakrishna's guidance; and his understanding of India and its people.[78] Vivekananda never quoted anything but the Vedas, the Upanishads and the Bhagavad Gita. Never did he try to claim ownership of his words.[79] When he turned into a *parivrajak* sanyasi at the age of 25, he relied on God and nothing else. He had given God—and God alone—complete control over his entire life.[80] He placed a greater value on serving Mother India than anything else, including his desire to stay in samadhi.[81]

After Vivekananda returned to India on 15 January 1897, the social service carried out by his followers accelerated significantly—whether it was relief work during the Calcutta

---

[76]Ibid., pp. 21–22.
[77]Sister Nivedita, *The Master as I Saw Him*, 9th ed., Kolkata: Udbodhan Office, 1962; 36th reprint, 2016, p. 40.
[78]Ibid., p. 65.
[79]Ibid., p. 15.
[80]Ibid., p. 21.
[81]Ibid., p. 33.

plague of 1899 or caring for cholera patients. Under his direction, projects such as the Varanasi hospital and the Murshidabad orphanage were also launched.[82] For him, service was worship:

> 'What the world wants today is twenty men and women who can dare to stand in the street yonder and say that they possess nothing but God. [...] What the world wants is character,' he says, in a letter written at this time to a member of his class. 'The world is in need of those whose life is one burning love—selfless. That love will make every word tell like a thunderbolt. Awake, awake, great souls! The world is burning in misery. Can you sleep?'[83]

Mahasamadhi

Vivekananda's health continued to deteriorate in his later days, yet his dedication to the cause was unwavering. Ultimately, due to a variety of factors, including his intense work schedule and physical stress, the Swami took 'mahasamadhi' at the Belur Math in Kolkata on 4 July 1902, when he was only 39 years old. It is said that he spent several hours meditating before leaving his mortal body and obtaining the highest level of nirvana. All the gurubhais and devotees were in a state of extreme shock. Swami Brahmananda's voice choked with tears, 'The Himalayas have disappeared

---

[82]Ibid., pp. 247–48.
[83]Ibid., pp. 21–22.

from view.'[84] After much grief, the body was ultimately carried to the funeral pyre where Swami Vivekananda and Sri Ramakrishna's names were passionately chanted. Sister Nivedita lit the pyre first, followed by the monks and numerous other people.[85]

---

[84]Dhar, Sailendra Nath, *A Comprehensive Biography of Swami Vivekananda Vol. 3*, Vivekananda Kendra Prakashan Trust, Chennai, 2012, p. 1986.
[85]Ibid., pp. 1979–92.

3

Spiritual Teachings

Swami Vivekananda's teachings respond to the timeless human quest for meaning, identity and purpose, rooted in a vision that empowers individuals to realize their inner potential and contribute meaningfully to society. His message was not limited to scholars or spiritual aspirants; it was a clarion call for the entire society—to rise in strength, awaken their inner divinity, and serve humanity with compassion and conviction. For Vivekananda, true spirituality was inseparable from action. He urged people to transcend fear, self-doubt and social divisions, and to lead lives of dignity, courage and service.

Rejecting ritualism, dogma and blind adherence to tradition, Vivekananda reinterpreted India's ancient wisdom in a manner that was both rational and practical. He believed that spiritual ideals must guide daily life, not remain confined to scriptures or discourses. His teachings championed a shift from weakness to strength, from passivity to purposeful action, and from a fragmented worldview to one rooted in oneness and interdependence. By linking the inner journey of self-discovery with the outer path of social responsibility, he offered a unique spiritual framework for modern times.

This chapter offers an exploration of Vedanta—the philosophical foundation of Vivekananda's worldview—and shows how Vivekananda brought its timeless principles to life through the language of science, service and self-realization. It then unfolds his core ideas: the inherent divinity of every soul, the unity of all human beings, the transformative power of thought, and the sacredness of service. In doing so, Vivekananda presents not just a spiritual doctrine, but a universal call to live with purpose, fearlessness and compassion, charting a path of inner freedom and collective upliftment.

Vedanta at the Core of Swami Vivekananda's Teachings

The core of Vivekananda's message to the world preaches the fundamental unity of existence. This emanates from his deep faith in the Vedantic understanding of life as manifested in the age-old wisdom of the Upanishads. He declared that all *darshan*s—schools of thought in India—ultimately derived their supreme authority from the Upanishads or Vedanta. Suggesting that all Indians should identify themselves as 'Vedantists', he proclaimed that 'whether we are conscious of it or not, we think the Vedanta, we live in the Vedanta, we breathe the Vedanta, and we die in the Vedanta.'[86]

---

[86] Swami Vivekananda, 'The Vedanta in All Its Phases', *The Complete Works of Swami Vivekananda Vol. III*, Advaita Ashrama, Uttarakhand, 2016, p. 338.

This context brings us to the fundamental question: what is the true essence of Vedanta or the Upanishadic tradition that Vivekananda was talking about? In his lecture 'The Vedanta', the Swami states that the central theme of the Upanishads is 'to find an ultimate unity of things. Knowledge is nothing but finding unity in the midst of diversity. Every science is based upon this; all human knowledge is based upon the finding of unity amid diversity.'[87]

Using this Vedantic framework, Vivekananda provided a scientific explanation of existence. He explained that the universe is a manifestation of a universal soul, which is spiritual in character and not constrained by the laws of matter. This universal being or soul, akin to our idea of God, is permanent, indestructible, mouldable, timeless and not limited by matter. Furthermore, every living thing possesses a soul that is inherently part of this greater universal soul, thus unfolding the true non-dualistic reality of the self and the absolute. The primary distinction between the two lies only in the degree of consciousness. Therefore, the *atman* (soul) within every living being—from the smallest seed to the largest beast—and the *paramatman* (universal soul) share the same inherent divinity.

Through these teachings, Swami Vivekananda preaches not only the importance of faith in oneself and the divine but also lays down a spiritual and practical roadmap for personal empowerment and national revival.

---

[87]Swami Vivekananda, 'The Vedanta', *The Complete Works of Swami Vivekananda Vol. III*, Advaita Ashrama, Uttarakhand, 2016, p. 411.

Contrasting Western and Indian Worldviews

Driven by his spirit of inquiry, Vivekananda highlighted the contrasting worldviews of India and the West. He observed that the Western mind tends to seek answers in the external world, while the Upanishadic traditions of India emphasize looking within. The Vedantic approach, therefore, does not limit itself to the finite and material aspects of life; instead, it encourages deep self-reflection to uncover answers to life's most profound and challenging questions. Vivekananda goes on to explain the dichotomy between the two outlooks in the following passage:

> Just as the Greek mind or the modern European mind wants to find the solution of life and of all the sacred problems of Being by searching into the external world. So did our forefathers, and just as the Europeans failed, they failed also. But the Western people never made a move more, they remained there, they failed in the search for the solution of the great problems of life and death in the external world, and there they remained, stranded; our forefathers also found it impossible, but were bolder in declaring the utter helplessness of the senses to find the solution. Nowhere else was the answer better put than in the Upanishad: यतो वाचो निवर्तन्ते अप्राप्य मनसा सह।
>
> —"From whence words come back reflected, together with the mind"; न तत्रचक्षुर्गच्छति न वाग्गच्छति—"There the eye cannot go, nor can speech reach."[88]

---

[88]Swami Vivekananda, 'The Vedanta in All Its Phases', *The Complete Works of Swami Vivekananda Vol. III*, Advaita Ashrama, Uttarakhand, 2016.

Meeting of Science and Spiritualism: Exchanges with Nikola Tesla

Vivekananda and Nikola Tesla may have first connected at an event hosted by the renowned French actress Sarah Bernhardt.[89] In one of the letters written from New York, dated 13 February 1896, Vivekananda wrote:

> Mr. Tesla was charmed to hear about the Vedantic Prâna and Âkâsha and the Kalpas, which according to him are the only theories modern science can entertain. Now both Akasha and Prana again are produced from the cosmic Mahat, the Universal Mind, the Brahmâ or Ishvara. Mr. Tesla thinks he can demonstrate mathematically that force and matter are reducible to potential energy. I am to go and see him next week, to get this new mathematical demonstration.[90]

In the diagram that follows, Vivekananda demonstrated the harmony between Vedantic theories and Western science.[91]

---

[89] *Tesla Memorial Society of New York*, 'Nikola Tesla and Swami Vivekananda', https://www.teslasociety.com/tesla_and_swami.htm. Accessed on 24 August 2023.
[90] Swami Vivekananda, 'Epistles-First Series—LVII', *The Complete Works of Swami Vivekananda Vol. V*, Advaita Ashrama, Uttarakhand, 2016, p. 97.
[91] *Tesla Memorial Society of New York*, 'Nikola Tesla and Swami Vivekananda', https://www.teslasociety.com/tesla_and_swami.htm. Accessed on 24 August 2023.

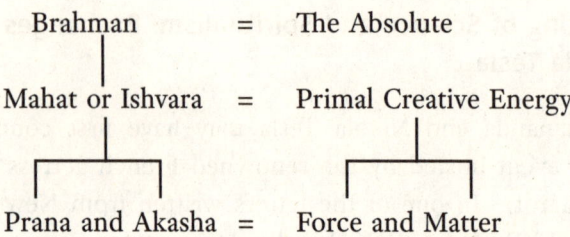

At a lecture delivered at Kumbakonam, Tamil Nadu, Vivekananda made a reference to his deliberations with Tesla and said that he 'would stand by the hour to attend my lectures on the Vedanta; for, as he expresses it, they are so scientific, they so exactly harmonise with the aspirations of the age and with the conclusions to which modern science is coming at the present time.'[92]

Practical Vedanta

Vivekananda delivered a series of lectures in London in 1896 called 'Practical Vedanta'. He argued that while theories can be intellectually stimulating, they must also be practical and applicable. Thus, for Vedanta to be meaningful, it needs to influence how we live, integrate with our daily actions, and dissolve the artificial separation between spiritual life and worldly existence. Explaining the idea, the Swami says that the core message of Vedanta is oneness—one life, one existence and one essence binding all beings. By teaching oneness, Vedanta encourages individuals to see all aspects

---

[92]Swami Vivekananda, 'The Mission of the Vedanta', *The Complete Works of Swami Vivekananda Vol. III*, Advaita Ashrama, Uttarakhand, 2016, p. 200.

of life as interconnected, promoting a holistic approach that transforms both personal and societal interactions. Ultimately, the Swami calls for a practical experience of Vedanta that manifests in compassionate, harmonious living.

Explaining the practical usefulness of such philosophies, Vivekananda says:

> The Vedanta, therefore, as a religion must be intensely practical. We must be able to carry it out in every part of our lives. And not only this, the fictitious differentiation between religion and the life of the world must vanish, for the Vedanta teaches oneness—one life throughout.[93]

The Bhagavad Gita, particularly, illustrates this principle, teaching that intense activity, even on a battlefield, can coexist with inner tranquillity. Vivekananda rejected both passivity and passion as ends in themselves, advocating for action rooted in equanimity. He argued that the greatest work was done by those with calm and balanced minds, undisturbed by emotions such as anger or fear.

In essence, 'Practical Vedanta' teaches that spiritual realization is not an abstract ideal but a practical path accessible to all, regardless of one's life circumstances. It calls for self-awareness, calm action and a recognition of the unity that underlies all existence. The idea of weakness or sin is dismissed as an illusion, and the focus is on manifesting one's inherent strength and divinity.

---

[93]Swami Vivekananda, 'Practical Vedanta: Part I', *The Complete Works of Swami Vivekananda Vol. II*, Advaita Ashrama, Uttarakhand, 2016, p. 285.

Divinity of Soul

Vivekananda emphasized the divine nature of the soul, asserting that each person was already capable of exploring their divinity, irrespective of their caste, gender, religion or race. Drawing from Vedanta, he stated that every living soul was inherently part of a larger universal soul. This means that each of us possesses a divine element at our core. This divinity can be explored, realized and actualized, allowing every human being the potential to unlock limitless possibilities within themselves. To quote him: 'Ay, let every man and woman and child, without respect of caste or birth, weakness or strength, hear and learn that behind the strong and the weak, behind the high and the low, behind every one, there is that Infinite Soul, assuring the infinite possibility and the infinite capacity of all to become great and good.'[94]

He often quoted a verse of Srimad Bhagavad Gita, which reiterates that the soul is both birthless and deathless, thus urging individuals to believe in their own intrinsic divinity as the path to self-reliance.

नैनं छिन्दन्ति शस्त्राणि नैनं दहति पावक: ।
न चैनं क्लेदयन्त्यापो न शोषयति मारुत: ॥ [2.23]...

[*nainaṁ chhindanti śhastrāṇi nainaṁ dahati pāvakaḥ na chainaṁ kledayantyāpo na śhoṣhayati mārutaḥ*]

"This Self, weapons cannot pierce, nor fire can burn, water cannot wet, nor air can dry up. Changeless,

---

[94]Swami Vivekananda, 'The Mission of the Vedanta', *The Complete Works of Swami Vivekananda Vol. III*, Advaita Ashrama, Uttarakhand, 2016, p. 207.

all-pervading, unmoving, immovable, eternal is this Self of man." We learn according to the Gita and the Vedanta that this individual Self is also Vibhu, and according to Kapila, is omnipresent.[95]

In this context, Vivekananda explored the concept of evolution, comparing the Western scientific understanding of physical evolution with the deeper, spiritual perspective found in Indian philosophy. While the West, through figures like Darwin, attributed evolution to competition, natural selection and survival of the fittest, Vivekananda drew on the teachings of Patanjali to present a more profound view. He introduced the idea of 'the infilling of nature' to explain that evolution was not just about external forces shaping life but an unfolding of inherent potential from within. He said, 'If a Buddha is the one end of the change, the very amoeba must have been the Buddha also. If the Buddha is the evolved amoeba, the amoeba was the involved Buddha also.'[96]

The key message here is that every being, from the simplest organism to the highest saint, contains the same infinite energy and potential. The difference between a worm and a Buddha is not in their essential nature but in the degree to which their divine potential is manifested. Vivekananda emphasized that the Buddha was not simply the end result of evolution from an amoeba; rather, the amoeba already held within it the potential to become a Buddha.

This concept reinforces the Vedantic belief that every

---

[95]Swami Vivekananda, 'The Vedanta', *The Complete Works of Swami Vivekananda Vol. III*, Advaita Ashrama, Uttarakhand, 2016, pp. 419–20.
[96]Ibid., p. 421.

soul is inherently divine and limitless. The journey of life, therefore, is not about acquiring new qualities or becoming something different but about manifesting more of the infinite divinity that already exists within each one of us. The spiritual evolution of the soul mirrors the physical evolution of life forms, with the ultimate realization being that all living beings are fundamentally one, differing only in the degree to which they have expressed their divine nature. This idea forms the foundation of Indian spirituality, emphasizing unity, oneness and the boundless potential within every individual.

As Vivekananda said, 'All power is within you; you can do anything and everything. Believe in that, do not believe that you are weak; do not believe that you are half-crazy lunatics, as most of us do nowadays. You can do anything and everything without even the guidance of anyone. All power is there. Stand up and express the divinity within you.'[97]

Self-Belief and Faith in God

The first step towards actualizing our divine potential is self-belief. Vivekananda underlined this truth when he stated that 'the history of the world is the history of a few men who had faith in themselves, and it is faith which calls out divinity within.'[98] His call for self-belief acts as a rally

---

[97] Swami Vivekananda, 'The Work before Us', *The Complete Works of Swami Vivekananda Vol. III*, Advaita Ashrama, Uttarakhand, p. 299.
[98] Swami Vivekananda, 'Jnana And Karma', *The Complete Works of Swami Vivekananda Vol. VIII*, Advaita Ashrama, Uttarakhand, 2016, p. 222.

against external aids, challenging everyone to realize their own potential: 'You must be Rishis yourselves. You are also men as much as the greatest men that were ever born—even our Incarnations. What can mere book-learning do? What can meditation do even? What can the Mantras and Tantras do? You must stand on your own feet.'[99]

To strengthen self-belief, Vivekananda advised us to tap into the power of *shraddha* or deep faith. He stated, 'The idea of true Shraddha must be brought back once more to us, the faith in our own selves must be reawakened, and, then only, all the problems which our country face will gradually be solved by ourselves.'[100] Further expounding on the concept of shraddha, he declared, 'We want Shraddhâ, we want faith in our own selves. Strength is life, weakness is death. "We are the Âtman, deathless and free; pure, pure by nature. Can we ever commit any sin? Impossible!"—such a faith is needed. Such a faith makes men of us, makes gods of us. It is by losing this idea of Shraddha that the country has gone to ruin.'[101] This quote underscores the necessity of unwavering faith in oneself to rise above challenges and restore one's strength and integrity.

According to Vivekananda, if you strongly believe in yourself, you will become self-reliant and not dependent on

---

[99] Swami Vivekananda, 'Sannyasa: Its Ideal and Practice', *The Complete Works of Swami Vivekananda Vol. III*, Advaita Ashrama, Uttarakhand, 2016, p. 461.

[100] Swami Vivekananda, 'Conversations and Dialogues—I–IV Shri Surendra Nath Sen', *The Complete Works of Swami Vivekananda Vol. V*, Advaita Ashrama, Uttarakhand, 2016, p. 338.

[101] Ibid.

others for your own life. He said, 'Be free; hope for nothing from anyone. I am sure if you look back upon your lives you will find that you were always vainly trying to get help from others which never came. All the help that has come was from within yourselves. You only had the fruits of what you yourselves worked for, and yet you were strangely hoping all the time for help.'[102]

Equating self-belief with belief in the divine, he proclaims, 'faith, faith, faith in ourselves, faith, faith in God—this is the secret of greatness.'[103] According to Vivekananda, faith in our inherent divinity is paramount. For him, Vedanta revealed a profound truth: divinity is non-dualistic and encompasses both the individual soul and the universal energy, or God. By equating belief in oneself with belief in God, he underscored the intrinsic connection between self-belief and faith in the divine.

Conversely, Vivekananda also explained how lack of belief in self was akin to being an atheist. While explaining the ideal of Vedanta, he said, 'Faith in ourselves will do everything. I have experienced it in my own life, and am still doing so; and as I grow older that faith is becoming stronger and stronger. He is an atheist who does not believe in himself. The old religions said that he was an atheist who did not believe in God. The new religion says that he is the

---

[102]Swami Vivekananda, 'Practical Vedanta: Part II', *The Complete Works of Swami Vivekananda Vol. II*, Advaita Ashrama, Uttarakhand, 2016, p. 316.
[103]Swami Vivekananda, 'The Mission of the Vedanta', *The Complete Works of Swami Vivekananda Vol. III*, Advaita Ashrama, Uttarakhand, 2016, p. 205.

atheist who does not believe in himself.'[104]

At the same time, Vivekananda also cautioned against misplaced faith: 'Have faith in all the three hundred and thirty millions of your mythological gods, and in all the gods which foreigners have now and again introduced into your midst, and still have no faith in yourselves, there is no salvation.'[105]

Particularly addressing the youth, he expressed his vision and confidence in their potential: 'Young men, my hope is in you. Will you respond to the call of your nation? Each one of you has a glorious future if you dare believe me. Have a tremendous faith in yourselves, like the faith I had when I was a child, and which I am working out now. Have that faith, each one of you, in yourself—that eternal power is lodged in every soul—and you will revive the whole of India.'[106]

Fearlessness and Strength

One of the major pre-requisites for inculcating self-belief is to be fearless. Vivekananda put a special onus on the younger generation to be fearless and encouraged them to boldly march forward: 'Be bold and fear not. It is only in our scriptures that this adjective is given unto the Lord—Abhih, Abhih. We have to become Abhih, fearless, and our

---

[104] Swami Vivekananda, 'Practical Vedanta: Part I', *The Complete Works of Swami Vivekananda Vol. II*, Advaita Ashrama, Uttarakhand, 2016, p. 295.
[105] Swami Vivekananda, 'The Mission of the Vedanta', *The Complete Works of Swami Vivekananda Vol. III*, Advaita Ashrama, Uttarakhand, 2016, p. 205.
[106] Swami Vivekananda, 'The Future of India', *The Complete Works of Swami Vivekananda Vol. III*, Advaita Ashrama, Uttarakhand, 2016, p. 318.

task will be done. Arise, awake, for your country needs this tremendous sacrifice. It is the young men that will do it. The young, the energetic, the strong, the well-built, the intellectual—for them is the task.'[107]

Going back to his core inspiration drawn from the Upanishadic tradition, Vivekananda stated:

> Strength, strength is what the Upanishads speak to me from every page. This is the one great thing to remember, it has been the one great lesson I have been taught in my life; strength, it says, strength, O man, be not weak... Ay, it is the only literature in the world where you find the word 'Abhih' 'fearless', used again and again; in no other scripture in the world is this adjective applied either to God or to man. Abhih, fearless![108]

Vivekananda also emphasized the importance of a strong body. Discussing the connection between the body, mind and soul, he explained: 'If there is no strength in the body and mind, the Atman cannot be realised. First you have to build the body by good nutritious food—then only will the mind be strong. The mind is but the subtle part of the body. You must retain great strength in your mind and words.'[109]

---

[107] Swami Vivekananda, 'Address of Welcome Presented at Calcutta and Reply', *The Complete Works of Swami Vivekananda Vol. III*, Advaita Ashrama, Uttarakhand, 2016, p. 334.

[108] Swami Vivekananda, 'Vedanta in its Application to Indian Life', *The Complete Works of Swami Vivekananda Vol. III*, Advaita Ashrama, Uttarakhand, 2016, p. 252.

[109] Swami Vivekananda, 'Conversations and Dialogues—V', *The Complete Works of Swami Vivekananda Vol. VII*, Advaita Ashrama, Uttarakhand, 2016, p. 130.

In this light, he also defined what it meant to be a real 'hero' and proclaimed:

> "The earth is enjoyed by heroes"—this is the unfailing truth. Be a hero. Always say, "I have no fear." Tell this to everybody—"Have no fear." Fear is death, fear is sin, fear is hell, fear is unrighteousness, fear is wrong life. All the negative thoughts and ideas that are in this world have proceeded from this evil spirit of fear. This fear alone has kept the sun, air, and death in their respective places and functions, allowing none to escape from their bounds. [...] Therefore, I say, "Be fearless, be fearless."[110]

Oneness of Humanity

Vivekananda championed the profound oneness of the universe, and by extension, the unity of humankind. Explaining this concept from a scientific lens, he stated:

> You and I, the sun, moon, and stars are but little waves or waveless in the midst of an infinite ocean of matter; how Indian psychology demonstrated ages ago that, similarly, both body and mind are but mere names or little waveless in the ocean of matter, the Samashti; and how, going one step further, it is also shown in the Vedanta that behind that idea of the unity of the whole show, the real Soul is one.[111]

---

[110] Ibid.
[111] Swami Vivekananda, 'The Mission of the Vedanta', *The Complete Works of Swami Vivekananda Vol. III*, Advaita Ashrama, Uttarakhand, 2016, p. 203.

In the context of modern-day social discrimination, Vivekananda emphasized the divinity of all souls, declaring:

> The soul has neither sex, nor caste, nor imperfection. We believe that nowhere throughout the Vedas, Darshanas, or Purânas, or Tantras, is it ever said that the soul has any sex, creed, or caste. Therefore, we agree with those who say, "What has religion to do with social reforms?" But they must also agree with us when we tell them that religion has no business to formulate social laws and insist on the difference between beings, because its aim and end is to obliterate all such fictions and monstrosities.[112]

Thus, it underlines the principle that religion should have no locus standi in the creation or validation of social laws that differentiate on the basis of gender, race, geography or socio-economic status. Instead, the essence of religion, according to the universal doctrine of Vedanta, is to break these barriers and guide us toward the realization of the essential oneness of all human beings despite apparent differences.

Interestingly, Vivekananda compared equality with the idea of 'oneness' by asking:

> I see no two alike, yet we are all human beings. Where is this one humanity? I find a man or a woman, either dark or fair; and among all these faces I know that there is an abstract humanity which is common to all.

---

[112]Swami Vivekananda, 'What we Believe in', *The Complete Works of Swami Vivekananda Vol. IV*, Advaita Ashrama, Uttarakhand, 2016, p. 349.

I may not find it when I try to grasp it, to sense it, and to actualise it, yet I know for certain that it is there. If I am sure of anything, it is of this humanity which is common to us all. It is through this generalised entity that I see you as a man or a woman.[113]

Here, he differentiated between idealistic notions of equality and the practical, enriching reality of diversity, while emphasizing the underlying unity that binds all humans.

Service as Worship to God

Vivekananda redefined the traditional understanding of God's worship. As a staunch advocate for the intrinsic divinity and unity of all living beings, he proposed that 'true worship' extended beyond the confines of temple rituals and mere deity adoration. According to Vivekananda, genuine worship involves recognizing 'Shiva' in every individual and treating all beings with reverence. Essentially, he taught that serving people around us was synonymous with serving God. This perspective was eloquently expressed during his address at the Rameswaram Temple where he said, 'He who sees Shiva in the poor, in the weak, and in the diseased, really worships Shiva; and if he sees Shiva only in the image, his worship is but preliminary. He who has served and helped one poor man seeing Shiva in him, without thinking of his caste, or creed, or race, or anything, with him Shiva is more pleased

---

[113]Swami Vivekananda, 'The Ideal of a Universal Religion', *The Complete Works of Swami Vivekananda Vol. II*, Advaita Ashrama, Uttarakhand, 2016, pp. 372–73.

than with the man who sees Him only in temples.'[114]

Vivekananda taught that 'oneness' is realized through selfless service to others, viewing them as extensions of oneself. He believed that 'the service of Jivas in a spirit of oneness' is the real manifestation of the inherent unity of all beings. This kind of service transcends individual differences, connecting us to a higher spiritual reality. By helping others as though we are serving ourselves, we manifest the Vedantic principle of oneness in everyday life.[115]

The Swami went as far as to label those who did not dedicate their lives to their fellow countrymen as 'traitors'— 'So long as the millions live in hunger and ignorance, I hold every man a traitor who, having been educated at their expense, pays not the least heed to them.'[116]

Importance of Thoughts

The Swami firmly believed in the power of thought. He asserted that our thoughts shape our reality—whether we view ourselves as strong, pure or free, or conversely, weak, impure or bound. He explains:

> Whatever you think, that you will be. If you think

---

[114]Swami Vivekananda, 'Address at the Rameswaram Temple on Real Worship', *The Complete Works of Swami Vivekananda Vol. III*, Advaita Ashrama, Uttarakhand, 2016, p. 157.

[115]Swami Vivekananda, 'Conversations and Dialogues—XV', *The Complete Works of Swami Vivekananda Vol. VII*, Advaita Ashrama, Uttarakhand, 2016, p. 189.

[116]Swami Vivekananda, 'Epistles-First Series—XXV', *The Complete Works of Swami Vivekananda Vol. V*, Advaita Ashrama, Uttarakhand, 2016, p. 57.

yourselves weak, weak you will be; if you think yourselves strong, strong you will be; if you think yourselves impure, impure you will be; if you think yourselves pure, pure you will be. This teaches us not to think ourselves as weak, but as strong, omnipotent, omniscient. No matter that I have not expressed it yet, it is in me. All knowledge is in me, all power, all purity, and all freedom. Why cannot I express this knowledge? Because I do not believe in it. Let me believe in it, and it must and will come out.[117]

Thus, belief in one's inner potential is essential for expressing the divinity and strength that already resides within. Vivekananda explained that by repeatedly thinking of ourselves as weak or limited, we degrade and bind ourselves. However, by thinking of ourselves as strong, free and powerful, we can reach our highest potential.

'I am low, I am low'—repeating these ideas in the mind, the man belittles and degrades himself. The *Shastra* (Ashtavakra Samhita, I.11) says:

मुक्ताभिमानी मुक्तो हि बद्धो बद्धाभिमान्यपि।
किम्वदन्तीह्सत्येयं या मति: सा गतिर्भवेत्।।

[*muktābhimānī mukto hi baddho baddhābhimāny api|
kiṁ vadantīha satyeyaṁ yā matiḥ sā gatiḥ bhavet ||*]

—"He who thinks himself free, free he becomes; he who thinks himself bound, bound he remains—this popular saying is true; as one thinks, so one becomes." He alone

---

[117] Swami Vivekananda, 'Vedantism', *The Complete Works of Swami Vivekananda Vol. III*, Advaita Ashrama, Uttarakhand, 2016, p. 146.

who is always awake to the idea of freedom, becomes free; he who thinks he is bound, endures life after life in the state of bondage. It is a fact. This truth holds good both in spiritual and temporal matters. Those who are always down-hearted and dispirited in this life can do no work; from life to life, they come and go wailing and moaning. "The earth is enjoyed by heroes"—this is the unfailing truth. Be a hero.[118]

While discussing the transformative power of thought, Vivekananda suggested the incorporation of a specific practice in our daily lives. In his words:

> "This Âtman is first to be heard of." Hear day and night that you are that Soul. Repeat it to yourselves day and night till it enters into your very veins, till it tingles in every drop of blood, till it is in your flesh and bone. Let the whole body be full of that one ideal, "I am the birthless, the deathless, the blissful, the omniscient, the omnipotent, ever-glorious Soul." Think on it day and night; think on it till it becomes part and parcel of your life. Meditate upon it, and out of that will come work.[119]

The key message is that through constant meditation on the idea that we are not limited beings but the omnipotent, ever-glorious soul, the awareness of our divine nature becomes an integral part of our being. By deeply internalizing this truth

---

[118]Swami Vivekananda, 'Conversations and Dialogues—V', *The Complete Works of Swami Vivekananda Vol. VII*, Advaita Ashrama, Uttarakhand, 2016, p. 130.

[119]Swami Vivekananda, 'Practical Vedanta: Part I', *The Complete Works of Swami Vivekananda Vol. II*, Advaita Ashrama, Uttarakhand, 2016, p. 295.

and through sustained focus on this ideal, our thoughts, actions and entire existence are elevated. Vivekananda believed that action naturally flowed from this awareness—when the heart is full of this divine realization, the work we perform is transformed and empowered by the infinite potential within. This teaching highlights the omnipotence of thought and the profound effect it has on shaping our reality, emphasizing that the realization and embodiment of our divine essence is the foundation of both spiritual and worldly success.

Contextualizing Ancient Wisdom

The most striking aspect of Vivekananda's teachings is how he contextualized the ancient wisdom of the Vedas, Upanishads, and the Srimad Bhagavad Gita to meet the needs of the modern age. He rejected the practice of blind adherence to tradition, instead encouraging individuals to apply logical reasoning and critical thinking in understanding and practising the timeless principles of Vedanta. His teachings were not meant to uphold rituals but to inspire a deeper understanding of life's purpose and the unity of all beings.

Vivekananda offered modern societies a transformative vision rooted in Vedanta's non-dualistic philosophy, which sees all people as expressions of a singular divine essence, transcending differences. For him, individual identities did not imply divisions; instead, they revealed the inherent divinity within each person. His message was grounded in his master's teaching that serving humanity is equal to serving God. He also stressed the power of thoughts, believing that they have the capacity to shape one's character, either building it up or breaking it down. To Vivekananda, the development of a strong, noble character was the foundation of both personal and spiritual growth.

The Swami's message varied according to his audience. In the West, he introduced the profound wisdom of India's civilizational heritage and knowledge traditions, presenting India's spiritual legacy to a new world. At home in India, his focus was on inspiring the younger generation to look within, awaken their inner strength and tackle the societal challenges of their time. He called upon them to spread the message of their civilization—'Divinity of the Soul', 'Oneness of Humanity', and 'Service as Worship to God'— to the world, while also striving for the liberation of their nation from colonial rule.

4

Impact on Modern-Day Leaders

From the earliest days of civilization, India has stood as a beacon of intellectual discourse and diverse philosophies. India's enduring legacy of debate and discourse showcases its commitment to intellectual freedom and diversity. In modern times, however, the nature of debate has undergone a significant change. Ideological imposition has become common, and every prominent leader has often been boxed into specific ideological categories, which are frequently used to advance various political agendas.

In this context, Vivekananda's philosophy emerges as a unifying force, inspiring and influencing leaders—past and present—across the ideological spectrum, transcending boundaries with his timeless message. His relentless efforts to spread the teachings of Vedanta have left an indelible mark on global thought. This chapter delves into the profound impact of his principles on pre- and post-Independence leaders, examining how his philosophy of universal oneness shaped their approach to leadership. It highlights how Vivekananda's teachings guided these leaders to navigate the complexities of leadership with a spirit of selfless service and unity.

A Cradle of Intellectual Freedom

Since the dawn of civilization, India has thrived as a vibrant hub for debate and intellectual exchange. The traditional concept of *shastrartha,* or intellectual debate, epitomizes this rich history. These debates, known for their heated yet principled nature, were traditionally centred on expansion of knowledge and sharing of perspectives rather than proving a point.

In contemporary times, however, the nature of debate has changed. Today, there is often a tendency to impose one's own ideology upon others. In contrast, the Bharatiya (Indian) approach values *anubhav* (experience)—learning, understanding, testing and ultimately living out the ideals. This commitment to experiential knowledge is a testament to India's quest for uncovering the truth.

India's ancient philosophical landscape is diverse, encompassing schools of thought such as Purva Mimansa, Uttar Mimansa (Vedanta), Nyaya, Vaisheshika, Sankhya and Yoga,[120] all of which uphold the ethical and the moral values put forth in the Vedas. In sharp contrast is the Charvaka school of thought, which advocated materialism and rejected Vedic principles. Charvaka, proponent of this alternative philosophy, was neither persecuted nor silenced, exemplifying India's enduring tradition of embracing diverse perspectives and fostering open, respectful discourse among differing viewpoints.

---

[120]See the section on 'Spiritual and Philosophical Terms' in the Glossary.

A Unifying Force in Times of Divisiveness

In an era increasingly marked by mistrust and ideological divide, the life and teachings of Swami Vivekananda offer a unifying path, bridging diverse societal perspectives. He once famously said, 'Love must conquer hatred, hatred cannot conquer itself.'[121] Vivekananda's message of universalism, strength, self-reliance and service to humanity transcends political, ideological and cultural boundaries, offering a meeting ground for all.

Over the recent decades, India's prominent leaders have often been pigeonholed into specific ideological categories, utilized to serve various political agendas. Whether aligned with the right, left or centre, Swami Vivekananda's philosophy emerges as a potential unifier. His teachings and persona have the potential to harmonize these seemingly disparate groups.

Vivekananda is often viewed through a narrow lens, but it is essential to understand his life and message as an integrated whole. Associating him with a particular ideology reveals only a superficial grasp of the profound depth of his legacy. His entire life was devoted to the service of mother India. As Sister Nivedita poignantly remarked, he 'breathed India'.[122] Vivekananda's philosophy, therefore, acts as a bridge between different ideologies, embodying the spirit of unity in diversity.

---

[121] Swami Vivekananda, 'The Work before Us', *The Complete Works of Swami Vivekananda Vol. III*, Advaita Ashrama, Uttarakhand, 2016, p. 292.
[122] Sister Nivedita, *The Master as I Saw Him*, 9th ed., Kolkata: Udbodhan Office, 1962; 36th reprint, 2016, p. 40.

Netaji Subhas Chandra Bose

The life of Subhas Chandra Bose, popularly known as Netaji, vividly illustrates the profound influence of Vivekananda's ideals. During a period of internal struggle, Netaji discovered his writings at a neighbour's house. After reading just a few pages, he realized that he had found what he was missing all along. Netaji would often discuss the teachings of Vivekananda and his guru, Ramakrishna, with his wide circle of friends.[123] His life was completely transformed by Vivekananda's teachings. In his book, titled *An Indian Pilgrim: An Unfinished Autobiography*, Netaji reminisced:

> I was barely fifteen when Vivekananda entered my life. Then there followed a revolution within and everything was turned upside down. It was, of course, a long time before I could appreciate the full significance of his teachings or the greatness of his personality, but certain impressions were stamped indelibly on my mind from the outset. Both from his portraits as well as from his teachings, Vivekananda appeared before me as a full-blown personality. Many of the questions which vaguely stirred my mind, and of which I was to become conscious later on, found in him a satisfactory solution.[124]

Netaji immersed himself in Vivekananda's writings and was particularly influenced by his lecture series titled

---

[123]Bose, Subhas Chandra, *An Indian Pilgrim: An Unfinished Autobiography*, Sisir Kumar Bose and Sugata Bose (eds.), Oxford University Press, 1997, pp. 39–58.
[124]Ibid., p. 38.

'Colombo to Almora'. Netaji concluded that the essence of Vivekananda's teachings is to realize the ultimate goal of life, that is, '*Atmano Mokshartham Jagathitaya Cha* (For the salvation of our individual self and the welfare of all in the world).'[125] This motto was crafted by Vivekananda himself and adopted by the Ramakrishna Mission.[126]

Netaji further stated:

> The intellectual doubt which assailed me needed satisfaction and, constituted as I then was, that satisfaction would not have been possible without some rational philosophy. The philosophy which I found in Vivekananda and in Ramakrishna came nearest to meeting my requirements and offered a basis on which to reconstruct my moral and practical life. It equipped me with certain principles with which to determine my conduct or line of action whenever any problem or crisis arose before my eyes.[127]

This relationship with Vivekananda's ideals, which began when Netaji was 15, endured throughout his life. He regularly read Vivekananda's writings, visited Ramakrishna Mission centres and meditated before the photos of Ramakrishna, Sarada Devi (Holy Mother) and the Swami. Even during his time in Cambridge, Netaji remained deeply influenced by

---

[125]Ibid., pp. 36–38
[126]Ramakrishna Math and Mission, 'About Us', https://tinyurl.com/yembhttb. Accessed on 29 March 2022.
[127]Bose, Subhas Chandra, *An Indian Pilgrim: An Unfinished Autobiography*, eds. Sisir Kumar Bose and Sugata Bose, Oxford University Press, 1997, p. 54.

Vivekananda's teachings, frequently mentioning him in his letters.[128] These teachings continued to inspire him during the freedom struggle, where he emerged as a key leader. Discussing the influence of Ramakrishna Paramhansa and Vivekananda on his life and work, Netaji wrote in his book *The Indian Struggle 1920–34*:

> In the eighties of the last century, two prominent religious personalities appeared before the public who were destined to have a great influence on the future course of the new awakening. They were Ramakrishna Paramhansa, the saint, and his disciple Swami Vivekananda. Ramakrishna, the master, was brought up in the orthodox Hindu fashion, but his disciple was a young man educated at the university who was an agnostic before he met the former. Ramakrishna preached the gospel of the unity of all religions and urged the cessation of inter-religious strife. He emphasised the necessity of renunciation, celibacy and asceticism in order to live a truly spiritual life. With him religion was the inspirer of nationalism. He tried to infuse into the new generation a sense of pride in India's past, of faith in India's future and a spirit of self-confidence and self-respect. Though the Swami never gave any political message, everyone who came into contact with him or his writings developed a spirit of patriotism and a political mentality.[129]

---

[128]Ibid., pp. 36, 37, 159, 169, 179.
[129]Bose, Subhas Chandra, *The Indian Struggle 1920–42*, Sisir Kumar Bose and Sugata Bose (eds.), Oxford University Press, New Delhi, 1997, p. 22.

Baba Saheb Ambedkar

Dr Bhimrao Ramji Ambedkar, one of India's greatest leaders, inspired millions with his tireless efforts to overcome the challenges of social discrimination. Renowned for his achievements across multiple disciplines, his contributions to social justice are celebrated not only in India but globally. Popularly known as Baba Saheb Ambedkar, his works are frequently included in university curriculum and continue to resonate with a diverse range of students.

Ambedkar had a high regard for Vivekananda. In a conversation with Mundapallil Oommen Mathai, popularly known as M.O. Mathai, Ambedkar had remarked, 'Buddha was the greatest soul India had ever produced.' He also said that the greatest man India produced in recent centuries was not Gandhi but Swami Vivekananda.[130]

Vivekananda's revolutionary message of equal dignity for all people, regardless of caste, creed or social status, clearly left a lasting impression on Ambedkar. For the Swami, every soul was inherently divine, and the best way to serve God was by serving humanity, particularly the most vulnerable. His travels across India and the world demonstrated this ideal, as he lived among beggars and the downtrodden, never discriminating based on caste, creed or gender. This ethos of equality and service deeply influenced Ambedkar's own vision of social justice.

Both Vivekananda and Ambedkar shared a profound admiration for the Buddha. Vivekananda often quoted the

---

[130]Mathai, M.O., *Reminiscences of the Nehru Age*, Vikas Publishing House, New Delhi, 1978, p. 25.

Buddha in his speeches and interactions, and at the World Parliament of Religions, he spoke extensively about Buddha and Buddhism. His deep reverence for the Buddha led many in the West to believe that he was a preacher of Buddhism. 'Buddha never bowed down to anything—neither Veda, nor caste, nor priest, nor custom. He fearlessly reasoned so far as reason could take him. Such a fearless search for truth and such love for every living thing the world has never seen.'[131] According to Vivekananda, Buddha 'was the greatest man who ever lived. He never drew a breath for himself. Above all, he never claimed worship. Buddha is not a man, but a state. I have found the door. Enter, all of you!'[132]

Mahatma Gandhi

Widely recognized for spreading the doctrine of *ahimsa* (non-violence) globally, Mohandas Karamchand Gandhi—popularly known as Mahatma Gandhi—embodies the journey of not only an individual but also represents an entire philosophical movement. Since India's Independence, his life, beliefs and mission have profoundly shaped the foundation of modern India. Regardless of one's opinion about his methods, Gandhi's unmatched contributions to shaping India's national identity are indisputable.

Mahatma Gandhi—revered as the 'Father of the Nation'—

---

[131] Swami Vivekananda, 'Inspired Talks—Friday, July 19', *The Complete Works of Swami Vivekananda Vol. VII*, Advaita Ashrama, Uttarakhand, 2016, p. 57.

[132] Swami Vivekananda, 'Excerpts from Sister Nivedita's Book—VIII The Temple Of Pandrenthan', *The Complete Works of Swami Vivekananda Vol. IX*, Advaita Ashrama, Uttarakhand, pp. 418–19.

was significantly influenced by Vivekananda. Interestingly, the year Gandhi left for South Africa to practise law (1893) was also the year Vivekananda departed for the US to attend the World Parliament of Religions. Gandhi first encountered Vivekananda's writings during his time in South Africa. It is documented that Gandhi read the book *Raja Yoga* written by Vivekananda.[133]

After returning to India in 1901, Gandhi wanted to meet Vivekananda.[134] He eagerly travelled to Belur Math for that purpose, but discovered that the latter was ill. Gandhi mentions this episode in his autobiography: 'Having seen enough of the Brahmo Samaj, it was impossible to be satisfied without seeing Swami Vivekanand. So with great enthusiasm I went to Belur Math, mostly, or maybe all the way, on foot. I loved the sequestered site of the Math. I was disappointed and sorry to be told that the Swami was at his Calcutta house, lying ill, and could not be seen.'[135]

In 1921, on the birth anniversary of Vivekananda, Gandhi delivered a special address at the headquarters of the Ramakrishna Mission in Belur Math. In his speech, he expressed his profound respect for the late Vivekananda. After studying many of Vivekananda's books, Gandhiji found a significant alignment between his own ideals and those of the Swami. He told the gathering that if Vivekananda

---

[133]Gandhi, M.K., *The Story of My Experiments with Truth,* Mahadev Desai (trans.), Navajivan Publishing House, Ahmedabad, 1940, p. 297.
[134]Gandhi, M.K., *The Collected Works of Mahatma Gandhi Vol. 56* (ebook), Publications Division Government of India, New Delhi, 1999, p. 82.
[135]Gandhi, M.K., *The Story of My Experiments with Truth,* Mahadev Desai (trans.), Navajivan Publishing House, Ahmedabad, 1940, p. 268.

were alive, he would have been a great asset to the national awakening. However, even in his absence, his spirit remained with them, urging them to strive for the establishment of swaraj.[136] He added, 'I have gone through his works very thoroughly, and after having gone through them, the love that I had for my country became a thousandfold. I ask you, young men, not to go away empty-handed, without imbibing something of the spirit of the place where Swami Vivekananda lived and died.'[137]

Speaking at the Ramakrishna Mission in Rangoon in 1929, Gandhi said:

> I want to tell you something about Ramakrishna Paramahamsa and his mission. He has left for us a great work. I have faith in his mission, and I would ask you to follow him. Wherever I go the followers of Ramakrishna invite me and I know their blessings are on my work. Ramakrishna Sevashrams and Hospitals are spread throughout India. There is no such place where their work is not being carried on a small or large scale. Hospitals are opened and the poor are given medicine and treatment. When I remember Ramakrishna's name I cannot forget Vivekananda. Sevashrams have been largely spread by Vivekananda's activity and it was he who made his Master known throughout the world.[138]

---

[136]Gandhi, M.K., *The Collected Works of Mahatma Gandhi Vol. 22* (ebook), Publications Division Government of India, New Delhi, 1999, p. 291.

[137]Swami Vivekananda, *My India: The India Eternal [1st ed.]*, Ramakrishna Mission Institute of Culture, Calcutta, 2019, p. 206.

[138]Gandhi, M.K., *The Collected Works of Mahatma Gandhi Vol. 45* (ebook), Publications Division Government of India, New Delhi, 1999, p. 235.

Jawaharlal Nehru

In understanding the deep impact Vivekananda had on some of India's most influential leaders, the reflections of Pandit Jawaharlal Nehru offer valuable insights. Two of the best sources to learn Nehru's views on Vivekananda are his books—*Glimpses of World History* (1934) and *The Discovery of India* (1946). In *Glimpses of World History*, Nehru highlights Vivekananda's unique form of nationalism: 'A famous disciple of Ramakrishna's was Swami Vivekananda, who very eloquently and forcibly preached the gospel of nationalism. This was not in any way anti-Muslim or anti-anyone else, nor was it the somewhat narrow nationalism... Vivekananda's nationalism was Hindu nationalism, and it had its roots in Hindu religion and culture.'[139] Nehru recognized that Vivekananda's approach was not divisive; instead, it was rooted in a broad, inclusive vision that drew strength from India's ancient heritage while embracing modern challenges.

In *The Discovery of India*, Nehru further praised Vivekananda's ability to synthesize the past and present, writing, 'Rooted in the past and full of pride in India's heritage, Vivekananda was yet modern in his approach to life's problems and was a kind of bridge between the past of India and her present.'[140] Nehru's words acknowledge the Swami's role as a dynamic force of renewal, connecting India's spiritual legacy with the need for progress and strength in

---

[139] Nehru, Jawaharlal, *Glimpses of World History*, 18th Impression. Jawaharlal Nehru Memorial Fund and Oxford University Press, New Delhi, 2003, p. 437.

[140] Nehru, Jawaharlal, *The Discovery of India*, Oxford University Press, 1989, New Delhi, originally published 1946, p. 187.

the modern world. He also emphasized the Swami's stress on the scientific and experimental nature of yoga, stating, 'Vivekananda, one of the greatest of the modern exponents of Yoga and the Vedanta, has laid repeated stress on the experimental character of Yoga and on basing it on reason.'[141]

Hansraj Rahbar

Hansraj Rahbar, an eminent leftist thinker, activist and writer, studied the works of Vivekananda and subsequently authored the book *Vivekananda: The Warrior Saint*. In the preface, Rahbar explains why a 'staunch Marxist' like himself wrote a book on the Swami. He describes Vivekananda as one of the greatest thinkers India has ever produced and notes, 'We leftists have committed the blunder of branding Vivekananda as a mere religious swami and throwing away his priceless contribution from the nationalist treasury.'[142] Reading Vivekananda, Rahbar says, is like 'swimming in the ocean of enlightenment. In my opinion it is not possible to be a true Marxist without understanding him.'[143]

While Rahbar's book sparks new debates and discussions, his message is clear: understanding Vivekananda requires reading his works in their entirety rather than selectively, as many writers tend to do. Rahbar emphasized that Vivekananda's real message was intended not just for India but the entire world, for whose welfare he was born.

Other Indian Leaders

---

[141]Ibid.
[142]Rahbar, Hansraj, *Vivekananda: The Warrior Saint [10th ed.]*, Vijay Goel English-Hindi Publisher, Delhi, 2009, p. 10.
[143]Ibid.

Nobel laureate Rabindranath Tagore, a renowned poet, philosopher, musician and painter, wrote, 'If you want to know India, study Vivekananda. In him everything is positive and nothing negative.'[144] In pre-Independence India, communist revolutionary M.N. Roy, one of the founders of the communist movement in India, is said to have visited the Ramakrishna Mission 'in his search for knowledge and truth.'[145] It was Vivekananda's teachings that inspired Roy to dedicate his life to the country at an early age.[146]

On the other end of the socio-political spectrum, Dr Keshav Baliram Hedgewar, the founder of Rashtriya Swayamsevak Sangh (RSS), and Madhavrao Sadashivrao Golwalkar, the second and longest-serving *sarsanghchalak* (head) of the RSS, were greatly influenced by Vivekananda's thoughts and work. Golwalkar was closely associated with the Ramakrishna Mission and had been a disciple of Swami Akhandananda,[147] who was the direct disciple of Ramakrishna Paramhansa and brother disciple of Vivekananda. Moreover, Eknathji Ranade, who served as RSS General Secretary from 1956 to 1962 and established the Vivekananda Kendra in 1972, was strongly inspired by Vivekananda's principles.[148]

Also, Prime Minister Indira Gandhi attended the

---

[144]Swami Vivekananda, *My India: The India Eternal [1st ed.]*, Ramakrishna Mission Institute of Culture, Kolkata, 2019, p. 196.

[145]Roy, Samaren, *M.N. Roy: A Political Biography*, Orient Longman, New Delhi, 1997, p. 2.

[146]Ibid., pp. 2–4.

[147]Shri Golwalkar Guruji, *Glimpses of a Great Soul*, https://tinyurl.com/mvjheyje. Accessed on 30 July 2025.

[148]Ranade, Eknath, *The Story of The Vivekananda Rock Memorial*, Vivekananda Kendra Prakashan Trust, Chennai, 2017, p. 93.

extended inaugural celebrations of the Vivekananda Rock Memorial in Kanyakumari in September 1970.[149] Going forward, it was during the prime ministerial tenure of Rajiv Gandhi that 12 January, Vivekananda's birth anniversary, was declared as 'National Youth Day'.[150]

Other pre-Independence leaders such as Bal Gangadhar Tilak and Chakravarti Rajagopalachari and former presidents of India Rajendra Prasad and Sarvepalli Radhakrishnan also openly acknowledged the impact of Vivekananda on their lives and mission.

> **Chance Encounter with Jamsetji Tata**
>
> Jamsetji Tata had an accidental meeting with Vivekananda while they were aboard the same steamer, travelling from Japan to the US. During this journey, Jamsetji shared his desire to bring the steel industry to India. In response, the 30-year-old Swami emphasized the importance of transitioning to manufacturing instead of simply trading raw materials. According to the Swami, it was necessary to develop material sciences within the country. This insightful advice left a lasting impression on Jamsetji.[151] This meeting is believed to have had a significant influence on the eventual establishment of one of India's leading scientific

---

[149] Ibid.

[150] Shiraz, Zarafshan, 'National Youth Day 2024: Date, history, significance and celebration', *Hindustan Times*, 12 January 2024, https://tinyurl.com/yr7rddxp. Accessed on 30 June 2022.

[151] The Ramakrishna Mission Institute of Culture, *History of Science in India: An Introduction*, Kolkata, 2015, pp. 9–10.

institutions, the Indian Institute of Science (IISc).[152] After a few years, Jamsetji decided to establish a fundamental science research institute in India. He wrote to Vivekananda on 23 November 1898, asking for his guidance:

Dear Swami Vivekananda,

I trust you remember me as a fellow-traveller on your voyage from Japan to Chicago. I very much recall at this moment your views on the growth of the ascetic spirit in India, and the duty, not of destroying, but of diverting it into useful channels.

I recall these ideas in connection with my scheme of a Research Institute of Science for India, of which you have doubtless heard or read. It seems to me that no better use can be made of the ascetic spirit than the establishment of monasteries or residential halls for men dominated by this spirit, where they should live with ordinary decency, and devote their lives to the cultivation of sciences – natural and humanistic.

I am of opinion that if such a crusade in favour of an asceticism of this kind were undertaken by a competent leader, it would greatly help asceticism, science, and the good name of our common country; and I know not who would make a more fitting general of such a campaign than Vivekananda.

Do you think you would care to apply yourself to the mission of galvanizing into life our ancient traditions in this

---

[152]*Indian Institute of Science,* https://tinyurl.com/yt8uenx4. Accessed on 3 July 2024.

> respect? Perhaps you had better begin with a fiery pamphlet rousing our people on this matter. I should cheerfully defray all the expenses of publication.
>
> With kind regards,
>
> I am, dear Swami,
>
> Yours faithfully,
> Jamsetji N. Tata
>
> 23rd November 1898
> Esplanade House, Bombay[153]

Dr A.P.J. Abdul Kalam

Leading scientist and former president of India Dr A.P.J. Kalam, too, was an ardent admirer of Vivekananda and participated in several events related to Vivekananda. On 12 January 2006, Dr Kalam attended the 'Youth Convention' organized on Vivekananda's birth anniversary (National Youth Day) at the Vivekananda Institute of Value Education and Culture in Porbandar, Gujarat. In his speech, Dr Kalam mentioned that he had studied many books on Vivekananda. He highlighted two particular lines by the Swami that impressed him the most—'My name should not be made prominent. It is my ideas that I want to be realised.'[154] He further quoted the Swami in his speech—'Blessed are the

---

[153]*A Meeting On Board the Empress of India*, https://tinyurl.com/s4x2r9fm. Accessed on 16 December 2023.
[154]Swami Nikhileswarananda, 'Lecture of Abdul Kalam on Birthday of Swami Vivekananda', *YouTube,* 5 June 2020, https://tinyurl.com/3vdjb38c. Accessed on 15 April 2024.

pure in heart, for they shall see God, this purity of heart will bring the vision of God. It is indeed the theme of the whole music of this universe. This thought has indeed influenced my conscience.'[155] In 2012, Dr Kalam addressed the youth at several gatherings organized as part of Swami Vivekananda's 150th birth anniversary celebrations[156] and encouraged them to embrace Vivekananda's message.[157]

Dr Manmohan Singh

Dr Manmohan Singh, the former prime minister of India, was also a great admirer of Vivekananda. While speaking at the commemoration of the 150th birth anniversary of Swami Vivekananda, Dr Manmohan Singh elaborated in detail the relevance of the Swami in modern India and urged Indians—irrespective of faith and cultural identity—to embrace the message of Swami Vivekananda. He said, 'While promoting the idea of the oneness of all religions, Vivekananda promoted with equal zeal the idea of the equality of all human beings. Therefore, he rejected colonialism and alien rule as an affront to human dignity. This message inspired a new generation of Indians who, on the one hand, were rediscovering their own

---

[155] Abdul Kalam, A.P.J., 'Address at The Youth Convention And Inauguration Of The Vivekananda Institute Of Value Education And Culture At Porbandar, Gujarat', 12 January 2006, https://tinyurl.com/mtwv3myt. Accessed on 29 July 2025.

[156] DeshGujaratHD, 'APJ Abdul Kalam speaking on Swami Vivekananda's 150th anniversary function in Gujarat', *YouTube,* 12 January 2012, https://tinyurl.com/5tyh39hc. Accessed on 15 April 2024.

[157] Ramakrishna Mission Vivekananda Memorial, 'Follow the Message of Swami Vivekananda for Success in life – Dr. Kalam', 18 January 2012, https://tinyurl.com/5hcws3uv. Accessed on 15 April 2024.

history, their own heritage, their own civilizational attributes and contributions and, at the same time, wished to be a part of the modern world on the basis of liberty, equality and fraternity. In celebrating the life and teachings of Swami Vivekananda we are not just paying tribute to the past. That would be the wrong way to honour this great son of India. I sincerely believe that the best tribute to Vivekananda would be to recognise the relevance of his teachings and his thoughts for the 21st century, for today's India, for tomorrow's India. I urge every young Indian, irrespective of faith and religion, to be inspired by such a man as they build their own future in this ancient land of ours.'[158]

Narendra Modi

Vivekananda's teachings had a profound impact on Narendra Modi, India's current prime minister, particularly during his formative years. In an interview, he recalled that while preparing for debate competitions in middle school, he loved using Vivekananda's quotes in his speeches. This early exposure to Vivekananda's thoughts and words sparked his interest in delving deeper into his philosophy. Modi affirms that the Swami's ideas have played a pivotal role in shaping his worldview and continue to inspire him to date.[159] [160]

---

[158]Press Information Bureau, 'PM's address at the Closing Ceremony of the Commemoration of 150th Birth Anniversary of Swami Vivekananda', 12 January 2014, https://tinyurl.com/bdhjcxxm. Accessed on 26 July 2023.

[159]Modi, Narendra, 'Vivekananda's thoughts have inspired me since childhood', *YouTube*, 6 September 2016, https://tinyurl.com/4pampav9. Accessed on 23 February 2024.

[160]Modi, Narendra, 'Tough Line on Black Money: Full Text of PM Modi's Interview To Network 18', 2 September 2016, https://tinyurl.com/

During his tenure as the chief minister of Gujarat, Modi participated in numerous functions and programmes associated with Vivekananda. One notable example is the 'Swami Vivekananda Yuva Vikas Yatra', which he inaugurated on 11 September 2012.[161] After taking charge as the prime minister of the country, he continued his participation in programmes and events related to Vivekananda.

On 11 September 2017, PM Modi spoke in an event, 'Young India, New India', held to mark the 125th anniversary of Swami Vivekananda's historic address in Chicago in 1893. Speaking on the occasion, he remarked, 'If you look at it closely you'll see two aspects of Vivekanand Ji. Across the world wherever he went, wherever he got an opportunity to discuss, he would tirelessly glorify the great traditions and philosophy of India, he would never stop or feel embarrassed in doing so. That was one aspect. And the other aspect was whenever he would speak in India he would openly criticize our evil practices...During such a time and under such a condition, a young man of 30 years, stands up and says that you will not be able to reach God by following these rituals and worshiping in temples. He said, "Service to mankind is service to God." "Go and serve the poor and you will be able to reach God." What a great strength!'[162]

---

d79rh2kp. Accessed on 23 February 2024.

[161]Modi, Narendra, 'Glimpses of Day 1 of Vivekananda Yuva Vikas Yatra', 12 September 2012, https://tinyurl.com/44tucdy3. Accessed on 26 July 2023.

[162]Modi, Narendra, 'India is changing. India's standing at the global stage is rising and this is due to Jan Shakti: PM', 11 September 2017, https://tinyurl.com/mrhefavy. Accessed on 23 February 2024.

Since becoming the prime minister, Modi has visited the Belur Math (located within the greater Kolkata metropolitan area) several times. He also unveiled a statue of Vivekananda at Jawaharlal Nehru University in Delhi on 12 November 2020 through video conferencing.[163] In 2024, Modi visited the Vivekananda Rock Memorial in Kanyakumari for meditation.[164]

US Presidential Tribute to Swami Vivekananda

Swami Vivekananda's impact on America has woven his legacy into the fabric of US-India diplomatic relations. American presidents, including George Bush, Barack Obama and Donald Trump, have paid tribute to Vivekananda in their speeches during visits to India.[165]

On 27 January 2015, while speaking at the Siri Fort Auditorium in New Delhi, US President Barack Obama highlighted the enduring bond between the US and India by referencing Vivekananda's historic visit to America over 100 years ago. Vivekananda, who introduced Hinduism and yoga to the US, delivered a landmark speech in Chicago, touching on faith, the divine essence within each person and the

---

[163] Press Information Bureau, 'Prime Minister Shri Narendra Modi unveils statue of Swami Vivekananda at JNU Campus', 6 October 2022, https://tinyurl.com/yc38zhzu. Accessed on 24 October 2024.

[164] NDTV.Com, '"Feel A Divine Energy": PM Modi's Note After Meditating At Vivekananda Rock Memorial', 1 June 2024, https://tinyurl.com/4sf4k6wf. Accessed on 7 August 2024.

[165] Roy, Shubhajit, 'George Bush, Barack Obama, Donald Trump: Reading American Presidents India visit', *The Indian Express,* 28 February 2020, https://tinyurl.com/3d8jtv79. Accessed on 7 August 2024.

> purity of love. Obama recalled this moment with pride.[166]
>
> During this same visit, PM Modi and Obama jointly spoke on the radio programme *Mann ki Baat*. In this address, Modi fondly recalled his visit to the White House, where President Obama graciously acknowledged the cultural and spiritual significance of Swami Vivekananda. PM Modi recounted how Obama gifted him a book documenting Vivekananda's speeches from the World Religions Conference, highlighting his thoughtful understanding of Vivekananda's impact.[167]

Bringing People Together: Vivekananda Rock Memorial

In the Indian sociopolitical landscape, the left and right wings are often seen as adversaries. However, during the 1963 centennial celebration of Swami Vivekananda's birth, these ideological barriers did not hinder interactions among people with different political beliefs. At the time, Eknathji Ranade, an RSS member, was the organizing secretary of the Vivekananda Rock Memorial Committee. He sought support from leaders across the political spectrum—including the Congress Party, the different communist parties, Jan Sangh, DMK and the Republican Party—to help build the Vivekananda Rock Memorial at Kanyakumari. The memorial

---

[166]The White House, 'Remarks by President Obama in Address to the People of India', 27 January 2015, https://tinyurl.com/cbyd46aj. Accessed on 29 July 2025.

[167]Modi, Narendra, 'PM Modi and President Obama Share Their Thoughts Together on Mann ki Baat', 27 January 2015, https://tinyurl.com/yjj7yphd. Accessed on 29 July 2025.

was intended to commemorate the historical rock on which Swami Vivekananda meditated (between 25 and 27 December 1892) and found his life's mission after reflecting on the past, present and future of India.

After consulting veteran Congress leader Lal Bahadur Shastri, Eknath Ranade sought to gather signatures for a petition to construct the memorial. The petition was addressed to Prime Minister Jawaharlal Nehru. In a surprising feat, Eknath Ranade collected 323 signatures from the members of parliament in just three days, with almost every member present in Delhi signing the draft. He reached out to people from all ideologies and political parties, including Raghunath Singh, secretary of the Congress Parliamentary Party; Ram Manohar Lohia; N.G. Ranga; Atal Bihari Vajpayee; communist leader Renu Chakravarti; and DMK leaders such as V.R. Nedunchezhiyan and C.N. Annadurai. Annadurai was pleased with the plan and remarked, 'Vivekananda was a great man and, in fact, the entire country is indebted to him for his ideas and if they really accepted anybody, it was Vivekananda.'[168]

Pleased with the support for the project, Eknath Ranade stated, 'To my great satisfaction, I found that almost all people belonging to various political groups responded to the call and that they had complete identification with Vivekananda's Idea, with whatever Vivekananda had said. It was a great revelation to me.'

Eknath Ranade formed state-level committees and enlisted some other political stalwarts from across parties

---

[168] Ranade, Eknath, *The Story of The Vivekananda Rock Memorial*, Vivekananda Kendra Prakashan Trust, Chennai, 2017, p. 28.

and ideologies to collect money for the construction of the memorial. Meenakshisundaram Kalyanasundaram, a prominent leader of the Communist Party of India in Madras, was aware that such a committee was being formed in Tamil Nadu. He had presumed that no one would approach him because of his affiliation with the communist party. So, when he saw Eknath Ranade at his doorstep, he was pleasantly surprised. Kalyanasundaram said, 'I am happy you have come. You see, I am an admirer of Vivekananda. I was moulded by Vivekananda. In my younger days, when I was a student, I used to read his lectures, passage after passage and get inspired. From what he said here, there, in America and England, we got our lessons on patriotism.'[169]

Eknath Ranade also approached Jyoti Basu, a distinguished leader of the Communist Party of India (Marxist). At the time, Basu was the deputy chief minister of West Bengal. Ranade invited him to serve as one of the vice presidents of the West Bengal committee for the Vivekananda Rock Memorial. Initially, Basu declined and said, 'I have nothing to do with Vivekananda.'[170] But Ranade said, 'How can I believe that you can't have anything to do with him? Did he not stand for the oppressed? You stand for the oppressed. He stood for the downtrodden, you stand for the downtrodden. How can I believe if you or anybody who says you have nothing to do with Swami Vivekananda?'[171] Basu said, 'Yes, in that way, I am his admirer as he stood for the oppressed and the downtrodden. But with the spiritual

---

[169]Ibid., p. 64.
[170]Ibid., p. 65.
[171]Ibid., p. 66.

aspect of his life, I don't have any connections whatsoever.'[172]

Eknath Ranade replied, 'That may be true. So what? Of all the national heroes, if you accept him as a hero, it does not mean that you should accept all that he said in his life. I will not accept many things. You will not accept many things. But then he stood for the oppressed and for the downtrodden. He worked for the masses and infused confidence in them.'[173]

Basu was convinced but needed his party's approval to become the vice president of the committee. The permission was, however, denied by his party. Despite this, his belief in Vivekananda's mission led him to offer his trade union contacts for fundraising. Ranade also approached Kamala Basu, Jyoti Basu's wife, who was not a communist party member. After assurances that it was just a fundraising drive, she raised ₹1,100 from her network.[174]

These accounts illustrate that meaningful outcomes can be achieved when dialogue is conducted with openness and is free from prejudice or bias. If an RSS worker could successfully engage and garner support from those with opposing ideologies, then surely we can come together on matters of national importance. While political differences are inevitable, ideological divides should never obstruct the unifying message of Vivekananda, who championed practical spirituality, selfless service and the oneness of humanity.

---

[172]Ibid.
[173]Ibid.
[174]Ibid., p. 68.

Vivekananda Kendra—Spiritually-Oriented Service Mission

In 1972, Eknathji Ranade established Vivekananda Kendra, a mission dedicated to promoting Swami Vivekananda's spiritual teachings and service. Run by committed volunteers, the organization seeks to uphold Vivekananda's legacy through various service-oriented initiatives. With over 850 branches and activity centres across India, Vivekananda Kendra focuses on national regeneration. Its programmes encompass moral and cultural education, rural development, sustainable resource management, youth and women's empowerment and publications on Vivekananda's teachings, Indian culture and Vedic studies. These efforts play a vital role in strengthening the nation's social fabric and preserving its cultural heritage.[175]

---

[175]Vivekanada Rock Memorial & Vivekananda Kendra, 'Vivekananda Kendra—Spiritually Oriented Service Mission', https://tinyurl.com/yu2jj3vm. Accessed on 23 February 2024.

5

Relevance in the Contemporary World

*Don't care, be fearless. O brave one,
here I am by your side!*[176]

What sets Swami Vivekananda apart as a truly exceptional and transformative leader is his insistence that spirituality should not be confined to intellectual debate but must be lived and applied in everyday life. Unlike other spiritual leaders, he urged people to use the principles of Vedanta as a practical tool to address society's pressing challenges. His vision transcended theoretical discussions, making spirituality a force for real change in the world.

Today, as the world continues to confront issues such as social injustice, gender discrimination, religious intolerance, identity politics, global conflicts and deeper existential questions about life's purpose and personal

---

[176]Swami Vivekananda, 'Epistles-Fourth Series—CXI Rakhaln', *The Complete Works of Swami Vivekananda Vol. VIII*, Advaita Ashrama, Uttarakhand, p. 410.

well-being, Vivekananda's universal teachings continue to offer meaningful solutions. His timeless wisdom addresses both the external and internal struggles we face, making his insights as impactful now as they were then.

A significant portion of the population, particularly the youth, continues to face internal challenges related to purpose, mission and direction in life. Questions often arise about how to channel one's energy, which path to follow and how to deal with the overwhelming number of options or the lack thereof. Additionally, mental health issues, which always existed, have gained heightened attention, especially in the post-COVID era. Swami Vivekananda not only offered theoretical guidance on controlling the mind but also provided practical lessons to achieve mental well-being. Alongside mental health, physical health has also emerged as a major concern for all ages, and Vivekananda, a passionate advocate of sports, emphasized physical well-being as the foundation for accomplishing anything in life.

Vivekananda also addressed social challenges faced by women during that time, many of which remain relevant to this day. He highlighted the discrimination women endure solely due to their gender and emphasized that they must have the autonomy to decide their own future, free from external pressures. He firmly believed that the upliftment of women was essential for the upliftment of the nation, famously comparing the nation to a bird that cannot soar with one strong wing and one weak wing. His vision continues to offer a practical path toward gender parity.

Furthermore, issues of caste and identity have become deeply entrenched in society, often leading to division and polarization. The politicization of caste has weakened the nation. In this context, Vivekananda's message of unity, equality and social harmony is more relevant than ever, offering a vital roadmap to navigate these challenges and restore societal balance.

This chapter explores these and other key issues, demonstrating how Vivekananda's timeless teachings provide both practical solutions and profound guidance in addressing the pressing challenges of the contemporary world.

Maker of Your Own Destiny

Each day, life tests us with different questions and challenges. Every other moment feels like appearing for an exam where we are expected to give our best. But often, we feel helpless, as though the available paths lead nowhere, and we are falling down an endless rabbit hole. These challenges could manifest as the pressure to clear exams, find a job, get married, or even grapple with larger existential questions such as life's purpose. At such times, many of us experience the human urge to blame others for our own circumstances. Alternatively, we tend to overtly rely on others to find solutions for our own challenges.

Vivekananda particularly warned us against the habit of blaming others for our own failures. He said, 'Why? We complain of others in our failures. The moment I am unsuccessful, I say so-and-so is the cause of the failure. In failure, one does not like to confess one's own faults and weaknesses. Each person tries to hold himself faultless and lay the blame upon somebody or something else, or even on bad luck.'[177] This message is especially relevant during such crucial moments of our lives when we are called to look inward and draw upon the strength of our own character.

The same principle applies to physical fitness or our social relationships. We cannot change our destiny overnight. Our outcomes are a result of numerous daily routines and the little steps we take every day. In relationships, we often become overly dependent on a single person, thereby getting trapped in an endless loop of expectations. However, this does not happen accidentally; it is a result of continuous actions taken over a period of time. Our inability to solve our life's problems arises because we rely too heavily on others. But if we recognize that we are the creators of our own destiny, hope never ceases to exist. Reliance on the power of self gives us a reason to find a way to rise again. Therefore, any form of complete dependency should be seen as poisonous. To sum it up in the words of Swami Vivekananda:

> Those that blame others—and, alas! the number of them is increasing every day—are generally miserable with helpless brains; they have brought themselves to that pass through their own mistakes and blame others, but this does not alter their position. It does not serve them in any way. This attempt to throw the blame upon others only weakens them the more. Therefore, blame none for your own faults, stand upon your own feet, and take the whole responsibility upon yourselves.[178]

---

[177] Swami Vivekananda, 'The Powers of the Mind', *The Complete Works of Swami Vivekananda Vol. II*, Advaita Ashrama, Uttarakhand, 2016, p. 14.
[178] Swami Vivekananda, 'Jnana-Yoga', *The Complete Works of Swami*

Goal Orientation

For many young people, figuring out what they want to do in life feels like an endless game. Most of us move through each day without a clear perspective or direction. Yet, life needs a guiding theme—one that aligns with a larger purpose. Without a sense of purpose, we live in disconnected episodes where our intentions and actions fail to synchronize. A lack of purpose leaves us scattered, with too much to worry about and not enough to focus on. However, with a clear purpose, our thoughts and actions come into harmony, allowing us to achieve focus and direction. As Vivekananda suggested: 'Take up one idea. Make that one idea your life—think of it, dream of it, live on that idea. Let the brain, muscles, nerves, every part of your body, be full of that idea, and just leave every other idea alone. This is the way to success, and this is the way great spiritual giants are produced. Others are mere talking machines.'[179]

This leads us to the next question: What idea is really worth fighting for?

It does not matter which belief systems we adhere to. The real question is not about deciding which path is good or bad for us or which ideology we should adopt. Instead, we must ask ourselves how committed we are to pursuing our dreams. How much of ourselves are we willing to sacrifice for an idea? Are we willing to hold on to a thought over a period of time? For one minute, one hour, one day, one

---

Vivekananda Vol. II, Advaita Ashrama, Uttarakhand, 2016, pp. 220–21.
[179] Swami Vivekananda, 'Pratyahara and Dharana', *The Complete Works of Swami Vivekananda Vol. I*, Advaita Ashrama, Uttarakhand, 2016, p. 175.

week, one month, two months, one year, several years, a decade or a lifetime? Ultimately, it is not the idea itself that matters most but the extent of our dedication and the sacrifices we are prepared to make in order to realize it.

The founder of Vivekananda Kendra, Eknathji Ranade, describes choosing one path as equivalent to rejecting a million other paths. According to him:

> Choosing involves rejection, outright rejection. If you are to choose what you must do, once you choose your purpose, once you set your eyes on the goal of life, purpose of life, the mission of life, what you are going to do in this life then you will not be confused. If you do not choose you will be confused.[180]

Once the purpose is decided, we must focus on the means to an end. Look at the end but focus on the means too. Energy needs to be invested in the process; hence, we must design our own paths. According to Vivekananda:

> One of the greatest lessons I have learnt in my life is to pay as much attention to the means of work as to its end. [...] We forget that it is the cause that produces the effect; the effect cannot come by itself; and unless the causes are exact, proper, and powerful, the effect will not be produced. [...] When the cause is there, there is no more difficulty about the effect, the effect is bound to come. If we take care of the cause, the effect

---

[180] Bhide, Nivedita Raghunath (ed.), *Spiritualizing Life: Book Form of the Talks of Eknathji Ranade,* Vivekananda Kendra Prakashan Trust, Chennai, 2017, p. 93.

will take care of itself. The realization of the ideal is the effect. The means are the cause: attention to the means, therefore, is the great secret of life.[181]

On our journey, we must actively reject anything that weakens us in any way. Whether knowingly or unknowingly, various factors can drain our strength and make us feel powerless and hopeless. It is essential to identify these influences early on, as they can hollow us out from within. These factors could range from a habit or a relationship to a social circle or even a device. Vivekananda aptly said, 'Anything that makes you weak physically, intellectually, and spiritually, reject as poison; there is no life in it, it cannot be true. Truth is strengthening. Truth is purity, truth is all-knowledge; truth must be strengthening, must be enlightening, must be invigorating.'[182] The journey from confusion to clarity is long and challenging, but it can be truly rewarding for those who are willing to sacrifice everything for their goal.

Mental Well-Being

In modern times, mental well-being is often viewed through the lens of overcoming disorders like depression and anxiety. However, Vivekananda's teachings offer a more holistic understanding of mental health, emphasizing the mind's hidden potential. According to Vivekananda, true mental

---

[181] Swami Vivekananda, 'Work and its Secret', *The Complete Works of Swami Vivekananda Vol. II*, Advaita Ashrama, Uttarakhand, 2016, pp. 1–2.
[182] Swami Vivekananda, 'My Plan of Campaign', *The Complete Works of Swami Vivekananda Vol. III*, Advaita Ashrama, Uttarakhand, 2016, p. 239.

well-being involves not just managing stress or emotions but unlocking the deeper mysteries of our consciousness.

Vivekananda believed that understanding the mind was key to understanding the universe itself. He used the metaphor of clay to illustrate this idea: 'If I know one lump of clay, I know the whole mass of clay.' In other words, the universe is constructed on the same principles, and the individual—like a lump of clay—is a part of this larger whole. By knowing the human soul—which Vivekananda likened to a single atom—we can grasp the broader workings of nature. Birth, growth, decay and death follow the same cycle in all forms of life, whether in a plant or a human being. Although the timeline may vary, the process remains universal. For Vivekananda, the only reliable way to analyse the universe was through the study of our own minds.[183]

He further explained that our perception of the world is always filtered through the mind. Whatever we perceive or understand about life is not purely objective but rather a combination of our consciousness and the external environment. Referring to the ancient sage Kapila, Vivekananda said, 'The greatest psychologist the world has ever known, Bhagavan Kapila, demonstrated ages ago that human consciousness is one of the elements in the makeup of all objects we perceive, both internal and external.'[184] From our physical bodies to the highest spiritual truths, every perception is a mix of our consciousness and

---

[183]Swami Vivekananda, 'Introduction to Jnana-Yoga', *The Complete Works of Swami Vivekananda Vol. VI*, Advaita Ashrama, Uttarakhand, 2016, p. 42.
[184]Swami Vivekananda, 'The Philosophy of Ishvara', *The Complete Works of Swami Vivekananda Vol. III*, Advaita Ashrama, Uttarakhand, 2016, p. 44.

something external. This blend of subjectivity and external reality shapes what we commonly refer to as 'truth'.

Vivekananda, therefore, rejected the notion of pure objectivity. Our perception of good or bad is inherently subjective, shaped by the mind's interpretations. As he said, 'We have seen that it is the subjective world that rules the objective. Change the subject, and the object is bound to change. Purify yourself, and the world is bound to be purified.'[185] This insight is especially relevant today when we often focus on fixing others rather than addressing our own shortcomings. According to Vivekananda, the world will change only when we change ourselves. If we cultivate purity within, we will perceive purity outside. He asked, 'Why should I see evil in others? I cannot see evil unless I be evil. I cannot be miserable unless I am weak.'[186]

In essence, Vivekananda urged us to focus on purifying our own minds. Rather than projecting negativity onto others—which may simply reflect our inner turmoil—he advocated for inward transformation as the path to improving our interactions with the world.[187]

The key takeaway from Vivekananda's teachings is that by knowing and mastering our minds, we gain the power to reshape our perception of reality. He used the analogy of the hydrostatic paradox to explain this concept: 'One drop of water can balance the universe.' Just as a tiny engine can

---

[185] Swami Vivekananda, 'Vedanta And Privilege', *The Complete Works of Swami Vivekananda Vol. I*, Advaita Ashrama, Uttarakhand, 2016, p. 416.
[186] Ibid., p. 416.
[187] Swami Vivekananda, 'Concentration: Its Practice', *The Complete Works of Swami Vivekananda Vol. I*, Advaita Ashrama, Uttarakhand, 2016, p. 257.

reveal problems in a larger system, our inner world (the microcosm) influences the outer world (the macrocosm). If we adjust ourselves internally, the external world will adjust accordingly. In this way, our understanding and mastery of the mind become the foundation for transforming both our individual lives and the larger universe.[188]

Physical Health

As the world grapples with a tsunami of lifestyle diseases, stress and unhealthy habits, today's youth are once again searching for ways to improve their physical health and return to a disciplined, healthy life. In this context, Vivekananda, a 19th-century monk, emerges as a unique messenger who prioritized physical health even before talking about religion or any higher ideals. At a time when the concept of physical or public health received little attention, Vivekananda's focus on the subject seemed almost blasphemous. He boldly stated:

> First of all, our young men must be strong. Religion will come afterwards. Be strong, my young friends; that is my advice to you. You will be nearer to Heaven through football than through the study of the Gita. These are bold words; but I have to say them, for I love you. I know where the shoe pinches...[189]

---

[188] Swami Vivekananda, 'Inspired Talks—Wednesday, July 3', *The Complete Works of Swami Vivekananda Vol. VII*, Advaita Ashrama, Uttarakhand, 2016, p. 27.
[189] Swami Vivekananda, 'Vedanta in its Application to Indian Life', *The Complete Works of Swami Vivekananda Vol. III*, Advaita Ashrama,

Throughout his interactions with people, Vivekananda laid a special emphasis on physical health. He spoke at length about how a healthy body and a stable mind must accompany any worthwhile endeavour. He asked, 'How will you struggle with the mind unless the physique be strong?'[190] Clarifying his position, Swami Vivekananda explained that only with a strong and healthy body could one achieve control over one's mind. And once this stage of mind-body unison was achieved, the realization of self would follow more naturally. 'First build up your own physique. Then only you can get control over the mind. "नायमात्माबलहीनेनलभ्यः— this Self is not to be attained by the weak" (Katha Upanishad, I.ii.23).'[191]

Practising what he preached, Vivekananda relied on his physical strength to journey across the length and breadth of the country. With minimal resources, he often travelled on foot, occasionally using bullock carts, or by train when someone offered to buy his tickets. His robust physique enabled him to endure the challenging task despite varying weather and external conditions. Talking about his own physical discipline, he says, 'Don't you find me exercising every day with dumb-bells even now? Walk in the morning and evenings and do physical labour. Body and mind must run parallel.'[192]

Uttarakhand, 2016, p. 257.

[190] Swami Vivekananda, 'Conversations and Dialogues—VIII', *The Complete Works of Swami Vivekananda Vol. VII*, Advaita Ashrama, Uttarakhand, 2016, p. 148.

[191] Ibid., p. 149.

[192] Swami Vivekananda, 'Conversations and Dialogues—X', *The Complete Works of Swami Vivekananda Vol. VII*, Advaita Ashrama, Uttarakhand, 2016, p. 164.

The Calcutta plague offers another lens to explore Vivekananda's perspective on public health. Between 1898 and 1899, Calcutta was struck by a plague that affected a significant portion of its population. Coming to the rescue of the local people, Vivekananda and the Ramakrishna Mission carried out relief work. Interestingly, Vivekananda drafted a 'Plague Manifesto', which outlined a detailed list of dos and don'ts for controlling the spread of the disease and managing the associated panic. His guidance was remarkably ahead of its time, particularly in light of the recent global experience with the COVID-19 pandemic.

THE PLAGUE MANIFESTO

Om Salutations to Bhagavan Shri Ramakrishna

Brothers of Calcutta!

We feel happy when you are happy, and we suffer when you suffer.

If that grave disease—fearing which both the high and the low, the rich and the poor are all fleeing the city—ever really comes in our midst, then even if we perish while serving and nursing you, we will consider ourselves fortunate because you are all embodiments of God. He who thinks otherwise— out of vanity, superstition or ignorance—offends God and incurs great sin. There is not the slightest doubt about it.

We humbly pray to you—please do not panic due to unfounded fear.

Come, let us give up this false fear and, having faith in the infinite compassion of God, gird our loins and enter the field of action. Let us live pure and clean lives. Disease, fear of an epidemic, etc., will vanish into thin air by His grace.

(a) Always keep the house and its premises, the rooms, clothes, bed, drain, etc., clean.

(b) Do not eat stale, spoiled food; take fresh and nutritious food instead. A weak body is more susceptible to disease.

(c) Always keep the mind cheerful. Everyone will die once. Cowards suffer the pangs of death again and again, solely due to the fear in their own minds.

(d) Fear never leaves those who earn their livelihoods by unethical means or who cause harm to others. Therefore, at this time when we face the great fear of death, desist from all such behaviour.

(e) During the period of epidemic, abstain from anger and from lust—even if you are householders.

(f) Do not pay any heed to rumours.

(g) The British government will not vaccinate anyone by force. Only those who are willing will be vaccinated.

(h) There will be no lack of effort in treating the afflicted patients in our hospital under our special care and supervision, paying full respect to religion, caste and the modesty (Purdah) of women. Let the wealthy run away! But we are poor; we understand the heartache of the poor. The Mother of the Universe is Herself the support of the helpless. The Mother is assuring us: "Fear not! Fear not!"

7. Brother, if there is no one to help you, then send information immediately to the servants of Shri

> Bhagavan Ramakrishna at Belur Math. There will be no dearth of help that is physically possible. By the grace of the Mother, monetary help will also be possible.[193]

Women's Rights

'There is no chance for the welfare of the world unless the condition of women is improved. It is not possible for a bird to fly on only one wing.'[194] Swami Vivekananda's deep respect for women's rights was shaped by his early life experiences—he was deeply influenced by his mother and Maa Sarada, the spiritual partner of Ramakrishna Paramhansa. Sister Nivedita recounts how Vivekananda recognized the pivotal role women played in society:

> The Temple of Dakshineshwar was built by the wealthy Rani Rashmani, a woman of the Koiburto caste, and in the year 1853, Sri Ramakrishna took up his residence there, as one of the Brahmins attached to its service. These were facts which had impressed the mind of Vivekananda even more deeply, perhaps, than he himself ever knew. A woman of the people had been, in a sense, the mother of that whole movement of which all the disciples of his Master formed parts. Humanly

---

[193] Swami Vivekananda, 'The Plague Manifesto', *The Complete Works of Swami Vivekananda Vol. IX*, Advaita Ashrama, Uttarakhand, 2016, pp. 330–32.

[194] Swami Vivekananda, 'Epistles-Second Series—LXXV Shashi', *The Complete Works of Swami Vivekananda Vol. VI*, Advaita Ashrama, Uttarakhand, 2016, p. 336.

speaking, without the Temple of Dakshineshwar there had been no Ramakrishna, without Ramakrishna no Vivekananda, and without Vivekananda, no Western Mission.[195]

Reflecting on the historical status of women in the Indian society, Vivekananda stated:

> [The] idea of the Aryans is the freedom of women. It is in the Aryan literature that we find women in ancient times taking the same share as men, and in no other literature of the world. [...] There is not one passage throughout the whole mass of literature of the Vedas which can be construed even indirectly as signifying that woman could never be a priest. In fact, there are many examples of women officiating as priests. [...] There is another point which I bring before you and where the Hindu woman is still superior to all other women in the world—her rights. The right to possess property is as absolute for women in India as for men—and has been for thousands and thousands of years. If you have any lawyer friend and can take up commentaries on the Hindu law, you will find it all for yourselves.[196]

He also talked about women in leadership roles and remarked:

---

[195] Sister Nivedita, *The Master as I Saw Him*, 9th ed., Kolkata: Udbodhan Office, 1962; 36th reprint, 2016, p. 234.
[196] Swami Vivekananda, 'The Women of India', *The Complete Works of Swami Vivekananda Vol. IX*, Advaita Ashrama, Uttarakhand, 2016, pp. 208–14.

Women in statesmanship, managing territories, governing countries, even making war, have proved themselves equal to men—if not superior. In India I have no doubt of that. Whenever they have had the opportunity, they have proved that they have as much ability as men, with this advantage—that they seldom degenerate. They keep to the moral standard, which is innate in their nature. And thus as governors and rulers of their state, they prove—at least in India—far superior to men. John Stuart Mill mentions this fact.[197]

Swami Vivekananda's famous words further articulate his stance on gender equality in the modern context: 'No man shall dictate to a woman; nor a woman to a man. Each one is independent. What bondage there may be is only that of love. Women will work out their own destinies— much better, too, than men can ever do for them. All the mischief to women has come because men undertook to shape the destiny of women.'[198] His message underscored the importance of agency and independence for women, emphasizing that they alone should shape their future.

The only responsibility Vivekananda placed on the society is to educate women and explained, 'Our right of interference is limited entirely to giving education. Women must be put in a position to solve their own problems in their own way. No one can or ought to do this for them. And our Indian women are as capable of doing it as any in the world.'[199] He further

---

[197]Ibid., pp. 218–19.
[198]Swami Vivekananda, 'My Life And Mission', *The Complete Works of Swami Vivekananda Vol. VIII*, Advaita Ashrama, Uttarakhand, 2016, p. 86.
[199]Swami Vivekananda, 'On Indian Women–Their Past, Present And

urged parents to prioritize their daughters' education, saying, 'Educate your women first and leave them to themselves; then they will tell you what reforms are necessary for them. In matters concerning them, who are you?'[200]

> **Sister Nivedita Girls' School**
>
> Sister Nivedita Girls' School, now known as the Ramakrishna Sarada Mission Sister Nivedita Girls' School, was inaugurated by Sri Sarada Devi on 13 November 1898 in the company of Swami Vivekananda and his brother disciples. Initially, the school commenced as a provisional establishment and transitioned into a fully operational educational institution by 1902.[201]

In conclusion, Swami Vivekananda's perspective on gender reflects a profound humanism, best captured in his own words: 'We should not see ourselves as men or women, but as human beings, destined to care for and support one another'—a timeless call to transcend gender divisions and uphold the dignity and unity of all.[202]

Future', *The Complete Works of Swami Vivekananda Vol. V*, Advaita Ashrama, Uttarakhand, 2016, p. 223.

[200] Swami Vivekananda, 'Notes Taken Down in Madras, 1892–93', *The Complete Works of Swami Vivekananda Vol. VI*, Advaita Ashrama, Uttarakhand, 2016, p. 124.

[201] *Ramakrishna Sarada Mission Sister Nivedita Girls School*, (n.d.), https://tinyurl.com/427cmeaj. Accessed on 29 July 2025.

[202] Swami Vivekananda, 'Sayings and Utterances', *The Complete Works of Swami Vivekananda Vol. V*, Advaita Ashrama, Uttarakhand, 2016, p. 414.

Caste and Social Justice

Vivekananda's views on the caste system were shaped by his extensive readings of ancient and contemporary texts, the society in which he was raised and his travels across India and other countries. He made a clear distinction between caste and religion, emphatically arguing that caste is a social institution rather than a religious one. He expressed this distinction by saying: 'Do I believe in caste? Caste is a social custom; religion has nothing to do with it; all castes will associate with me.'[203]

Vivekananda explained that the caste system originally emerged as a social order organized around the different occupations people undertook. However, he opposed any special privileges granted to those from higher castes and was equally against the discrimination faced by those from lower castes. Advocating for the eventual breakdown of the caste system, he said, '[T]he caste system is opposed to the religion of the Vedanta. Caste is a social custom, and all our great preachers have tried to break it down. From Buddhism downwards, every sect has preached against caste, and every time it has only riveted the chains. Caste is simply the outgrowth of the political institutions of India; it is a hereditary trade guild. Trade competition with Europe has broken caste more than any teaching.'[204]

---

[203]Swami Vivekananda, 'Hindus at the Fair', *The Complete Works of Swami Vivekananda Vol. III*, Advaita Ashrama, Uttarakhand, 2016, p. 484.
[204]Swami Vivekananda, 'At The Twentieth Century Club of Boston', *The Complete Works of Swami Vivekananda Vol. V*, Advaita Ashrama, Uttarakhand, 2016, p. 316.

Vivekananda offered a transformative perspective on caste dynamics, advocating for the elimination of social distinctions through a Vedantic understanding of society, where every soul is inherently divine, underscoring the unity of humankind. He expressed his stance on caste structures by stating: 'I must frankly tell you that I am neither a caste-breaker nor a mere social reformer. I have nothing to do directly with your castes or with your social reformation. Live in any caste you like, but that is no reason why you should hate another man or another caste. It is love and love alone that I preach, and I base my teaching on the great Vedantic truth of the sameness and omnipresence of the Soul of the Universe.'[205]

In the Indian context, where caste-based discrimination and identity politics continue to influence both educational institutions and electoral democracy, Vivekananda's opinion is extremely relevant. His words serve as a timely reminder: 'Therefore, my friends, it is no use fighting among the castes. What good will it do? It will divide us all the more, weaken us all the more, degrade us all the more. The days of exclusive privileges and exclusive claims are gone, gone forever from the soil of India.'[206] This call is not for erasing identity but for transcending narrow self-interest in favour of collective upliftment grounded in spiritual equality. In the context of the resurgence of caste-based politics in

---

[205]Swami Vivekananda, 'The Mission of the Vedanta', *The Complete Works of Swami Vivekananda Vol. III*, Advaita Ashrama, Uttarakhand, 2016, pp. 208–09.

[206]Swami Vivekananda, 'The Future of India', *The Complete Works of Swami Vivekananda Vol. III*, Advaita Ashrama, Uttarakhand, 2016, p. 309.

educational institutions and electoral democracy in India, Vivekananda's advice continues to remain profoundly relevant and insightful.

Looking at the Swami's teachings from a broader lens offers a profound philosophical foundation for understanding and transcending social divisions such as caste, class, race and sectarianism. At the heart of his message lies the core Vedantic principle of the intrinsic oneness of all existence. 'For you must always remember that the one central ideal of Vedanta is this oneness. There is but one life, one world, one existence. Everything is that One, the difference is in degree and not in kind. The difference between our lives is not in kind.'[207] This declaration is not merely a spiritual insight but a radical social vision—one that renders artificial barriers meaningless in the light of the greater truth that all souls are essentially divine and interconnected.

For Vivekananda, the distinctions of caste and class were rooted not in reality, but in ignorance—born of misidentifying the outer form with the inner essence. A true Vedantist does not require separate theories to address caste, race or sectarian divides because all such distinctions dissolve in the recognition of the divinity that pervades all beings. His was a non-dualistic worldview where spiritual realization led directly to social harmony.

However, Vivekananda was also aware of the reality of the phenomenal world. He acknowledged that inequality exists in nature and society. But rather than accept it as

---

[207] Swami Vivekananda, 'Practical Vedanta: Part I', *The Complete Works of Swami Vivekananda Vol. II*, Advaita Ashrama, Uttarakhand, 2016, pp. 290–91.

inevitable or justified, he called upon individuals to rise above these distinctions through service, compassion and spiritual realization. If all are divine, then the highest milestone of equality is not just legal or social—it is spiritual. This makes his message especially relevant today. In a world fractured by divisions, Vivekananda's Vedanta offers a unifying template: to see all as one, to serve the divine in others, and to build a society rooted in the dignity and equality of all.

Religious Harmony

Religious intolerance is undeniably one of the most pressing issues facing the world today. From terrorism and ethnic genocide to global conflicts, inter-religious strife is an undeniable reality of our times. Often exacerbated by misinformation circulated on social media and deep-seated mistrust amongst communities, this tension is all too frequently exploited for political gain. What the world lacks, in this context, is a universal framework that not only rejects religious fanaticism but also provides equal respect and the right to practise one's faith freely without infringing upon others. It is in this challenging landscape that Vivekananda's teachings on religious tolerance resonate with an urgency that meets the current needs.

In his iconic address at the World Parliament of Religions in 1893, Vivekananda appealed for universal brotherhood. He proclaimed:

> Sectarianism, bigotry, and its horrible descendant, fanaticism, have long possessed this beautiful earth. They have filled the earth with violence, drenched

it often and often with human blood, destroyed civilization and sent whole nations to despair. Had it not been for these horrible demons, human society would be far more advanced than it is now. But their time is come; and I fervently hope that the bell that tolled this morning in honor of this convention may be the death-knell of all fanaticism, of all persecutions with the sword or with the pen, and of all uncharitable feelings between persons wending their way to the same goal.[208]

Vivekananda warned against the pitfalls of quarrelling over religious books and claiming superiority over one another based on one's scriptures. He urged people to look beyond differences and embrace a common humanity. Instead of relying on religious texts alone to build peace, he argued that the power of reason was the essential foundation for preventing inter-religious conflict. Vivekananda provocatively claimed, 'For it is better that mankind should become atheist by following reason than blindly believe in two hundred millions of Gods on the authority of anybody.'[209] This statement highlights his belief in the value of reasoned thought over blind adherence to religious dogma. He continued by asserting that 'no amount of books can help us become purer. The only power is in realization, and that lies in ourselves and comes from thinking. Let men think.'[210] Here, Vivekananda championed the transformative

---

[208] Swami Vivekananda, 'Response to Welcome', *The Complete Works of Swami Vivekananda Vol. I*, Advaita Ashrama, Uttarakhand, 2016, p. 4.
[209] Swami Vivekananda, 'Practical Vedanta: Part III', *The Complete Works of Swami Vivekananda Vol. II*, Advaita Ashrama, Uttarakhand, 2016, p. 328.
[210] Ibid.

power of personal realization and intellectual contemplation over blind obedience to religious authority.

His bold call for introspection and thoughtful realization, rather than an unthinking submission to scriptures, sets an extraordinary precedent. He envisioned a future where different religions would ultimately fuse into a 'union of philosophy', where each person is free to choose their teacher or form of worship as expressions of a shared unity. This vision of religious plurality, which respects diverse expressions of belief while maintaining a commitment to mutual understanding, reflects an inclusive approach to spirituality that remains deeply relevant today.[211]

Vivekananda's message of universal brotherhood holds religious tolerance as a paramount ideal. He argued that different religions were, in essence, diverse perspectives of the same truth, all converging on one 'universal truth', which he defined as the 'realisation of God'. Moving beyond tolerance alone, Vivekananda advocated for a 'Universal Religion' founded on harmony and brotherhood, one that embraced all faiths while celebrating their diversity. This vision provides a compelling template for achieving harmony in an increasingly polarized world.[212]

---

[211] Swami Vivekananda, 'Fundamentals of Religion', *The Complete Works of Swami Vivekananda Vol. IV*, Advaita Ashrama, Uttarakhand, 2016, p. 368.
[212] Swami Vivekananda, 'The Way to the Realisation of a Universal Religion', *The Complete Works of Swami Vivekananda Vol. II*, Advaita Ashrama, Uttarakhand, 2016, pp. 351–66.

6

Call to Action for India's Youth

Swami Vivekananda firmly believed that the youth possess the power to eradicate all evils, inequities and corruption, owing to their potential for transformative change. The youth, if guided properly, can set themselves free from the weight of deep-seated prejudices. The youth, with their energy, are capable of driving true transformation. He proclaimed, 'This is the time to decide your future—while you possess the energy of youth, not when you are worn out and jaded, but in the freshness and vigour of youth. Work—this is the time; for the freshest, the untouched, and un-smelled flowers alone are to be laid at the feet of the Lord, and such He receives. Rouse yourselves, therefore, or life is short.'[213]

Vivekananda presented specific duties to the youth, urging them to act for the rejuvenation of the nation. Despite being delivered more than 100 years ago, his message remains relevant to today's generation, and the duties he outlined are still crucial for addressing the challenges we face. Before focusing on these duties, Vivekananda stressed

---

[213] Swami Vivekananda, 'The Future of India', *The Complete Works of Swami Vivekananda Vol. III*, Advaita Ashrama, Uttarakhand, 2016, p. 318.

the importance of shedding two vices: laziness and jealousy, which he saw as crippling the masses. He observed that people had become lethargic, with both body and mind steeped in inactivity. To counter this, we need to develop a sense of urgency, precision and morality in all our endeavours. Additionally, he called for the elimination of jealousy, which serves no constructive purpose. The downfall of others does not benefit us, nor does their success diminish us; jealousy must be entirely eradicated from our hearts and minds.

Vivekananda's vision also demands renunciation; he made it clear that tyag and seva are the twin ideals of India. Everything we aspire to achieve as a nation necessitates giving up personal comfort for the welfare of others, which is the truest form of service to our motherland.

The Swami suggested that the past should serve as a guide for the future, highlighting that our history was not merely a story of struggle and defeat but one of resilience, perseverance and achievement. We have never been invaders nor sought to conquer others by force; instead, we possess a rich heritage and hold the oldest scriptures known to humanity. Therefore, we should draw upon the wisdom of our remarkable past to build a solid foundation for the future.

A key element of his message to the youth is the spread of education to every corner of the country. The right kind of education—one that blends secular knowledge with spiritual understanding—will cultivate inner strength and moral integrity in each individual. This education should resonate with national values and focus on character building, thereby empowering people to serve the greater good.

This chapter lays out these timeless assignments given by

Vivekananda to the youth—a vision of purposeful action, moral integrity and selfless service. They are as important today as they were when first delivered, urging each new generation to take up the challenge of nation-building, embracing the twin ideals of renunciation and service, and aspiring to make India a beacon of hope and unity for the entire world.

Foster an Organized Mindset

One of the most critical components of Vivekananda's vision for India's youth is the need to cultivate strong organization skills—a foundational requirement for the nation's progress. Vivekananda pointed out that one of the major shortcomings of Indian society was the absence of lasting organizational structures. He highlighted this by saying, 'In India, the one thing we lack is the power of combination, organisation, the first secret of which is obedience.'[214] He envisioned a future where, rather than relying on specific individuals, there would be a system that sustains itself: 'Set up such a machine as will go on automatically, no matter who dies or lives. We Indians suffer from a great defect, viz. we cannot make a permanent organisation—and the reason is that we never like to share power with others and never think of what will come after we are gone.'[215]

---

[214] Swami Vivekananda, 'Epistles-First Series—LXI Dr. Nanjunda Rao', *The Complete Works of Swami Vivekananda Vol. V*, Advaita Ashrama, Uttarakhand, 2016, p. 102.
[215] Swami Vivekananda, 'Epistles-Fourth Series—CXXXI Rakhal', *The Complete Works of Swami Vivekananda Vol. VIII*, Advaita Ashrama, Uttarakhand, 2016, p. 433.

During his travels in the West, Vivekananda witnessed the impressive results of organized efforts. He saw the capacity of Western societies to unify around common goals and urged Indians to learn from this. Reflecting on the power of collective will, he said, 'Why is it that organisations are so powerful? Do not say organisation is material. Why is it, to take a case in point, that forty millions of Englishmen rule three hundred millions of people here? What is the psychological explanation? These forty millions put their wills together and that means infinite power, and you three hundred millions have a will each separate from the other. Therefore, to make a great future India, the whole secret lies in organisation, accumulation of power, coordination of wills.'[216]

Vivekananda observed a major challenge within Indian communities—a tendency toward jealousy and an eagerness to lead without the willingness to follow. He noted, 'Here in India, everybody wants to become a leader, and there is nobody to obey. Everyone should learn to obey before he can command. There is no end to our jealousies; and the more important the Hindu, the more jealous he is. Until this absence of jealousy and obedience to leaders are learned by the Hindu, there will be no power of organisation. We shall have to remain the hopelessly confused mob that we are now, hoping and doing nothing.'[217]

For India to tap into the power of the collective,

---

[216] Swami Vivekananda, 'The Future of India', *The Complete Works of Swami Vivekananda Vol. III*, Advaita Ashrama, Uttarakhand, 2016, pp. 313–14.

[217] Swami Vivekananda, 'The Abroad and the Problems at Home', *The Complete Works of Swami Vivekananda Vol. V*, Advaita Ashrama, Uttarakhand, 2016, pp. 208–09.

Vivekananda urged the youth to abandon the desire for personal fame and to commit themselves to a greater cause. His rallying call was one of self-sacrifice and unwavering dedication: 'Act on the educated young men, bring them together, and organise them. Great things can be done by great sacrifices only. No selfishness, no name, no fame, yours or mine, nor my Master's even! Work, work the idea, the plan, my boys, my brave, noble, good souls—to the wheel, to the wheel put your shoulders! Stop not to look back for name, or fame, or any such nonsense. Throw self-overboard and work. Remember, "The grass when made into a rope by being joined together can even chain a mad elephant."'[218]

Today's youth have the opportunity to realize the Swami's vision by coming together with purpose, pooling their efforts and working toward the common good, free from personal ambition. His call to action remains as vital and relevant as ever, offering a blueprint for harnessing the power of collective goodness.

Broadcast Education to the Masses

For Vivekananda, education was not confined to individual improvement; he envisioned it as a tool for uplifting entire communities from poverty and ignorance. In a letter from Darjeeling to Sarala Ghosal, editor of *Bhârati*, on the topic of 'The Education that India Needs', the Swami wrote:

---

[218]Swami Vivekananda, 'Epistles-Fourth Series—X Alasinga', *The Complete Works of Swami Vivekananda Vol. V*, Advaita Ashrama, Uttarakhand, 2016, pp. 34–35.

'Education, education, education alone! Travelling through many cities of Europe and observing in them the comforts and education of even the poor people, there was brought to my mind the state of our own poor people, and I used to shed tears. What made the difference? Education was the answer I got.'[219]

While describing India's ancient education system, Vivekananda stated that its sole aim was holistic development, in stark contrast to the Western system, which focused on rote memorization of facts and information. In his lecture 'The Future of India', Vivekananda emphasized that 'if education is identical with information, the libraries are the greatest sages in the world, and encyclopedias are the Rishis.' And hence, true education must go beyond mere accumulation of information and focus on education that is 'life-building', 'man-making', 'character-making assimilation of ideas' and built on 'national lines'.[220]

In a letter to the Maharaja of Mysore from Chicago, dated 23 June 1894, he highlighted the importance of mass education, particularly for the oppressed classes, stating, 'The only service to be done for our lower classes is to give them education, to develop their lost individuality. That is the great task between our people and princes. Up to now nothing has been done in that direction. Priest-power and foreign conquest have trodden them down for centuries,

---

[219] Swami Vivekananda, 'The Education that India Needs', *The Complete Works of Swami Vivekananda Vol. IV*, Advaita Ashrama, Uttarakhand, 2016, p. 480.

[220] Swami Vivekananda, 'The Future of India', *The Complete Works of Swami Vivekananda Vol. III*, Advaita Ashrama, Uttarakhand, 2016, pp. 316–17.

and at last the poor of India have forgotten that they are human beings.'

Vivekananda stressed that education must be accessible to even the poorest citizens, adding: 'Now if the mountain does not come to Mohammed, Mohammed must go to the mountain. If the poor boy cannot come to education, education must go to him.' He envisioned an organized approach in which self-sacrificing sanyasis could travel from village to village, not only teaching religion but also imparting secular knowledge. 'Suppose two of these men go to a village in the evening with a camera, a globe, some maps, etc. They can teach a great deal of astronomy and geography to the ignorant. By telling stories about different nations, they can give the poor a hundred times more information through the ear than they can get in a lifetime through books.'

However, he acknowledged the challenges to this vision, particularly financial ones, lamenting, 'It is very difficult to set a wheel in motion; but when once set, it goes on with increasing velocity.' After struggling to gain support in India, he sought aid abroad but was disappointed with the Western apathy. He observed, 'The Americans do not care a bit whether the poor of India die or live. And why should they, when our own people never think of anything but their own selfish ends?'

Vivekananda issued a powerful call to action: to broadcast education across the length and breadth of the country, reminding us that 'this life is short, the vanities of the world are transient, but they alone live who live for others; the rest are more dead than alive.'[221]

His call for youth to spread transformative education through every corner of India is as relevant today as ever, urging us to commit wholeheartedly to the upliftment of society. Vivekananda's vision challenges us to look beyond personal success and to view education as a means for empowering entire communities, fostering unity and progress across the nation.

Cultivate Renunciation and Service

Swami Vivekananda identified 'renunciation' and 'service' as the national ideals for India. 'Renunciation, or tyag, calls for letting go of personal desires and attachments, while service, or seva, emphasizes selfless dedication to the welfare of humanity at large. Together, these ideals form the spiritual foundation of India.'[222]

Vivekananda's vision of service transcends the idea of offering assistance that is merely transactional or driven by self-interest. It embodies the higher spirit of seva—selfless service performed without any expectation of reward. Reflecting on the true essence of seva, Swami Vivekananda calls upon Indians to dedicate themselves fully to the service and upliftment of their nation. For the next 50 years, he

---

[221] Swami Vivekananda, 'Our Duty to the Masses', *The Complete Works of Swami Vivekananda Vol. IV*, Advaita Ashrama, Uttarakhand, 2016, pp. 353–55.

[222] Swami Vivekananda, 'Reawakening of Hinduism on a National Basis', *The Complete Works of Swami Vivekananda Vol. V*, Advaita Ashrama, Uttarakhand, 2016, p. 221.

urged, the foremost duty should be to revere 'our great Mother India' above all else. In warning against 'vain gods', Vivekananda pointed to the misdirected notions of worship that distract from this higher duty. Instead, he exhorted Indians to realize that 'the only God that is awake is our own race—everywhere, His feet, everywhere, His hands, everywhere, His ears, He covers everything.' True worship, he taught, began with honouring the Virat—the living, universal form manifest in our fellow beings and our land. Only after serving this living divinity, he affirms, will we be truly prepared to worship all other forms of God.[223]

The Swami underscored that before aspiring to spiritual heights or advanced practices like becoming a 'yogi' or engaging in deep meditation, one must first practise *'chittashuddhi'*—purification of the mind. He insisted that the most fundamental form of worship is selfless service to those around us. That is true devotion to the Virat, the universal form of godliness visible in our fellow countrymen and creatures. Instead of seeking distant ideals or different paths, he argued, Indians must first come together to serve the nation, shedding jealousy and division in favour of unity and compassion.

Vivekananda highlighted that the struggles and sufferings in India stemmed from this very 'karma'—the consequences of ignoring one another's humanity and competing rather than collaborating. Only by worshipping the 'God that we see all around us' and addressing the needs of the nation

---

[223]Swami Vivekananda, 'The Future of India', *The Complete Works of Swami Vivekananda Vol. III*, Advaita Ashrama, Uttarakhand, 2016, p. 315.

will Indians cultivate the spiritual and social strength needed for greater progress. In his vision, the true path to all other goals begins with selfless dedication to the well-being and unity of India and her people.[224]

For Vivekananda, this path to greatness required sacrifice. 'No great work has been done in the world without sacrifice. Who on seeing the tiny sprout of the banyan can imagine that in course of time it will develop into a gigantic banyan tree?'[225] This reflects the enduring impact of even the smallest acts of sacrifice over time.

In his rallying call, Vivekananda urged, 'Wipe off this blot. Arise and awake! What matters it if this little life goes? Everyone has to die, the saint or the sinner, the rich or the poor. The body never remains for anyone. Arise and awake and be perfectly sincere. Our insincerity in India is awful; what we want is character, that steadiness and character that make a man cling on to a thing like grim death.'[226]

In this spirit, Vivekananda called upon us to transcend personal ambitions, embracing selflessness as a path to true service, character and unwavering commitment to the welfare of the nation.

---

[224]Ibid.
[225]Swami Vivekananda, 'Conversations and Dialogues—XVIII', *The Complete Works of Swami Vivekananda Vol. VII*, Advaita Ashrama, Uttarakhand, 2016, p. 207.
[226]Swami Vivekananda, 'The Vedanta', *The Complete Works of Swami Vivekananda Vol. III*, Advaita Ashrama, Uttarakhand, 2016, pp. 443–44.

Take Pride in India's Past

Why is history important? Why should people be aware of it? And why should we take pride in India's past? The Swami emphasized the need to study history to appreciate Indian heritage and understand the values India embodied as a nation. He was critical of the distorted narratives that focus on India's defeats, invasions and enslavement, and observed, 'For centuries people have been taught theories of degradation. They have been told that they are nothing. The masses have been told all over the world that they are not human beings. They have been so frightened for centuries, till they have nearly become animals.'[227]

Instead, Vivekananda urged Indians to take pride in their civilizational heritage, reminding them, 'This is the ancient land where wisdom made its home before it went into any other country.'[228] Speaking about the importance of learning from our past, he proposed that by reconnecting with the greatness of India's past, Indians could build back a brighter future. Speaking to the youth, he said, 'Our ancestors were great. We must first recall that. We must learn the elements of our being, the blood that courses in our veins; we must have faith in that blood and what it did in the past; and out of that faith and consciousness of past greatness, we must build an India yet greater than what she has been.' In his view, periods of decay were as natural as periods of growth,

---

[227] Swami Vivekananda, 'My Plan of Campaign', *The Complete Works of Swami Vivekananda Vol. III*, Advaita Ashrama, Uttarakhand, 2016. p. 238.
[228] Swami Vivekananda, 'The Future of India', *The Complete Works of Swami Vivekananda Vol. III*, Advaita Ashrama, Uttarakhand, 2016, p. 300.

and from them, new strength would emerge:

> A mighty tree produces a beautiful ripe fruit. That fruit falls on the ground, it decays and rots, and out of that decay springs the root and the future tree, perhaps mightier than the first one. This period of decay through which we have passed was all the more necessary. Out of this decay is coming the India of the future; it is sprouting, its first leaves are already out; and a mighty, gigantic tree, the Urdhvamula, is here, already beginning to appear; and it is about that that I am going to speak to you.[229]

In today's world, where media, politics and even global discourse are saturated with conflicting narratives, the Swami's call to take pride in India's civilizational history holds profound relevance. It reminds us to stay rooted in our heritage, understand our values, recognize our national character and draw strength from our unique spiritual foundation.

Have Faith in India's Future

For Vivekananda, his motherland was of paramount importance, encompassing everything he cherished. His mind and heart were consistently devoted to India throughout his darkest periods and the most joyful times. He strove to instill unwavering faith in India's future, believing that faith in oneself and in God would naturally lead to faith

---
[229]Ibid., p. 301.

in the nation. As he declared, 'I have done nothing as yet; you have to do the task. If I die tomorrow the work will not die. I sincerely believe that there will be thousands coming up from the ranks to take up the work and carry it further and further, beyond all my most hopeful imagination ever painted. I have faith in my country, and especially in the youth of my country.'[230]

Vivekananda urged the youth to embrace the belief that 'India's future is my future' and to work earnestly toward a vision where India's future shines as brightly as her glorious past. Rather than comparing ourselves to other nations, he inspired the youth to overcome personal inertia and jealousy, channelling their energy toward constructive efforts that uplift the nation. He focused on identifying and overcoming internal and external challenges and building a foundation that promotes unity and prosperity.

India has given us everything, the Swami insisted; it is our responsibility to nurture it and to carry forward his vision. As he passionately proclaimed over 125 years ago, 'I do not see into the future; nor do I care to see. But one vision I see dear as life before me: that the ancient Mother has awakened once more, sitting on Her throne rejuvenated, more glorious than ever. Proclaim Her to all the world with the voice of peace and benediction.'[231]

---

[230]Swami Vivekananda, 'Address of Welcome Presented at Calcutta and Reply Lectures', *The Complete Works of Swami Vivekananda Vol. III*, Advaita Ashrama, Uttarakhand, 2016, pp. 335–36.
[231]Swami Vivekananda, 'Reply to the Madras Address', *The Complete Works of Swami Vivekananda Vol. IV*, Advaita Ashrama, Uttarakhand, 2016, p. 344.

Conquer through Spirituality, Not Invasion and Conversion

Vivekananda's message to future generations of Indians is a call to make a lasting contribution to the world by spreading spiritual knowledge, and not through domination. He envisioned India's influence as a profound, peaceful force that would transcend borders and inspire humanity. As he explained, 'In this land of charity, let us take up the energy of the first charity, the diffusion of spiritual knowledge. And that diffusion should not be confined within the bounds of India; it must go out all over the world.' Vivekananda challenged the belief that Indian thought had only recently reached other lands and stated, 'Those that tell you that Indian thought never went outside of India, those that tell you that I am the first Sannyasin who went to foreign lands to preach, do not know the history of their own race.'

He described how different nations might further the political agenda through the 'blast of trumpets and the march of cohorts' or how secular knowledge may be pushed through 'fire and sword'. But in India's case, the gift of spiritual knowledge 'can only be given in silence like the dew that falls unseen and unheard yet bringing into bloom masses of roses.' This he perceived as the most important gift India has to offer to the world as 'her quota of spiritual power to the sum total of the progress of the world.'[232]

---

[232] Swami Vivekananda, 'My Plan of Campaign', *The Complete Works of Swami Vivekananda Vol. III*, Advaita Ashrama, Uttarakhand, 2016, pp. 236–37.

Using his own life as an example, Vivekananda discussed how the impact of his work got compounded because he disseminated the message of Indian spirituality in the West. Therefore, he urged Indians to forsake material ambitions in favour of their moral duty to share spiritual truths globally. He addressed the youth of India: 'Young men, I specially ask you to remember this. We must go out, we must conquer the world through our spirituality and philosophy. There is no other alternative, we must do it or die. The only condition of national life, of awakened and vigorous national life, is the conquest of the world by Indian thought.'[233]

India should share her spiritual knowledge with the world; 'Let the Persian or the Greek, the Roman, the Arab, or the Englishman march his battalions, conquer the world, and link the different nations together, and the philosophy and spirituality of India is ever ready to flow along the new-made channels into the veins of the nations of the world.' Unlike material conquests, which are often driven by political or economic motives, India's mission is driven by a deep commitment to spiritual enrichment. Vivekananda called this India's gift to humanity, declaring, 'India's gift to the world is the light spiritual.'[234]

---

[233] Swami Vivekananda, 'The Work before Us', *The Complete Works of Swami Vivekananda Vol. III*, Advaita Ashrama, Uttarakhand, p. 292.
[234] Swami Vivekananda, 'First Public Lecture in the East (Colombo)', *The Complete Works of Swami Vivekananda Vol. III*, Advaita Ashrama, Uttarakhand, 2016, p. 125.

India's Destiny: Spreading the Light of Spiritual Wisdom

Though deeply spiritual, Vivekananda's message emerges as a powerful call for nation-building and collective action towards India's progress. He urged each individual to see their personal growth as inseparably linked to the nation's growth, aligning personal interests with the nation's well-being, which he saw as the foundation of true patriotism. He stated, 'In the interest of one's own nation is one's own interest; in the well-being of one's own nation is one's own well-being.'[235]

According to Vivekananda, every nation has a unique destiny and mission, and India's purpose is to spread the message of oneness and selfless service within its borders and across the globe. In his words, 'each nation has a destiny to fulfil, each nation has a message to deliver, each nation has a mission to accomplish.'[236] He stressed that as long as a nation's mission remained intact, the nation would thrive despite obstacles: 'Each nation has a mission for the world. So long as that mission is not hurt, that nation lives, despite every difficulty. But as soon as its mission is destroyed, the nation collapses.'[237]

He described the distinct role that each nation played,

---

[235] Swami Vivekananda, 'Modern India', *The Complete Works of Swami Vivekananda Vol. IV*, Advaita Ashrama, Uttarakhand, 2016, p. 469.

[236] Swami Vivekananda, 'The Common Bases of Hinduism', *The Complete Works of Swami Vivekananda Vol. III*, Advaita Ashrama, Uttarakhand, 2016, p. 383.

[237] Swami Vivekananda, 'My Life And Mission', *The Complete Works of Swami Vivekananda Vol. VIII*, Advaita Ashrama, Uttarakhand, 2016, p. 71.

emphasizing that India's unique contribution to the world was her spiritual heritage: 'Each nation has its own part to play, and naturally, each nation has its own peculiarity and individuality with which it is born. Here in this blessed land, the foundation, the backbone, the life-centre is religion and religion alone.' While other nations might have prioritized wealth, politics or commerce, Vivekananda saw spirituality as the heart of India, the unifying force in her national life. He asserted:

> Let others talk of politics, of the glory of acquisition of immense wealth poured in by trade, of the power and spread of commercialism, of the glorious fountain of physical liberty; but these the Hindu mind does not understand and does not want to understand. Touch him on spirituality, on religion, on God, on the soul, on the Infinite, on spiritual freedom, and I assure you, the lowest peasant in India is better informed on these subjects than many a so-called philosopher in other lands.[238]

---

[238] Swami Vivekananda, 'Reply to the Address of Welcome at Ramnad', *The Complete Works of Swami Vivekananda Vol. III*, Advaita Ashrama, Uttarakhand, 2016, p. 163.

Conclusion

Swami Vivekananda, the greatest spiritual leader of modern India, dedicated his life to serving his motherland against political and cultural invasions. Despite a lifespan of less than 40 years (1863–1902) and only about a decade of active work (December 1892–July 1902), following his life-changing experience in Kanyakumari, Vivekananda's impact remains boundless. His contributions to the spiritual and cultural revival in India, as well as his introduction of Vedanta and yoga to the West, continue to resonate across generations.

His growing influence among the youth, even to this day, can be attributed to several factors. His visionary words, rooted in the ancient wisdom of the Vedas, Upanishads and the Bhagavad Gita, have an enduring appeal. He not only spoke of spirituality but practised it, initiating services for the underprivileged that demonstrated the application of his teachings. His life of purity and immense sacrifice served as a powerful inspiration, especially during a time when many Indians lacked confidence in their own ancient traditions. Vivekananda boldly declared to the world that India had a profound message of universal oneness to share. He had no personal ambitions but a singular desire to re-ignite India's spiritual mission of promoting the oneness of humanity.

The Swami was remarkably practical, always adapting

his message to suit his audience and presenting it within a modern context to address their concerns effectively. His extensive travels across India and his success in the West strengthened his understanding of different perspectives. What set him apart as a spiritual leader was his humility—he never claimed a godlike status. Instead, he taught that serving the poor and downtrodden is the highest form of worship and that the Vedantic truth of oneness should be embodied in daily life. As a champion of practical Vedanta, Vivekananda also introduced a scientific approach to Indian spirituality, encouraging the use of reason and thought to help people realize the universe's fundamental unity.

Understanding that any significant work or idea often passes through stages of 'ridicule, opposition, and then acceptance', Vivekananda knew that those ahead of their time would likely face misunderstanding and resistance.[239] He urged perseverance, reminding us that opposition is a natural part of the journey. Therefore, we must have unwavering faith in oneself and in the universal energy we conceive as 'God'. His resilience, faith and dedication to truth continue to inspire and guide those who follow his legacy.

Swami Vivekananda's message echoes with unwavering conviction: India, rooted in the wisdom of antiquity, stands on the threshold of a bright and glorious future—making her both one of the oldest and most promising civilizations.[240]

---

[239] Swami Vivekananda, 'Epistles-First Series—XLVII Maharaja of Khetri', *The Complete Works of Swami Vivekananda Vol. V*, Advaita Ashrama, Uttarakhand, 2016, pp. 87–88.

[240] Swami Vivekananda, 'Address of Welcome Presented at Calcutta and

Further, he emphasized the immense responsibility each individual carried in shaping the future of India. He urged people to work with the utmost dedication and commitment, as if the entire burden of the nation's progress rested on their shoulders. He said, 'Work as if on each of you depended the whole work. Fifty centuries are looking on you, the future of India depends on you. Work on.'[241] By invoking 'fifty centuries', he reminded them of India's long and rich history, implying that the legacy of the past and the hope for the future depended on their efforts. His call to 'work on' is a powerful motivation to continue striving for the betterment of the nation, regardless of the challenges faced.

In conclusion, Swami Vivekananda's life stands as a testament to truth and a deep, inclusive understanding of diverse ideologies, cultures and civilizations. Breaking free from societal limitations, he became a bridge between East and West, harmonizing science with spirituality. His faith in the youth was unwavering, urging them to place national welfare above all else and recognize that a nation's progress was intrinsically linked to individual growth. Swami Vivekananda's enduring legacy inspires us to overcome personal barriers and commit wholeheartedly to the greater good—not only for our nation but for humanity as a whole.

Reply', *The Complete Works of Swami Vivekananda Vol. III*, Advaita Ashrama, Uttarakhand, 2016, p. 303.

[241] Swami Vivekananda, 'To my Brave Boys', *The Complete Works of Swami Vivekananda Vol. IV*, Advaita Ashrama, Uttarakhand, 2016, p. 361.

Annexure

Major Lectures Delivered by Swami Vivekananda in India and the West

Every lecture and discourse delivered by Swami Vivekananda serves as a beacon of light for the human soul. His teachings continue to inspire and guide countless individuals across the globe. Listed below are some of the major lectures delivered by Swami Vivekananda in both India and the West:

West

1. 'Steps to Realisation' (A class lecture delivered in New York, 18 December 1895)
2. 'My Master' (Delivered in New York and England in 1896)
3. 'The Necessity of Religion' (Delivered in London, 7 June 1896)
4. 'Unity in Diversity' (Delivered in London, 3 November 1896)
5. 'The Cosmos: The Macrocosm' (Delivered in New York, 19 January 1896)
6. 'The Cosmos: The Microcosm' (Delivered in New York, 26 January 1896)

7. 'Practical Vedanta: Part I' (Delivered in London, 10 November 1896)
8. 'Practical Vedanta: Part II' (Delivered in London, 12 November 1896)
9. 'Practical Vedanta: Part III' (Delivered in London, 17 November 1896)
10. 'Practical Vedanta: Part IV' (Delivered in London, 18 November 1896)
11. 'Hints on Practical Spirituality' (Delivered at the Home of Truth, Los Angeles, California, 29 December 1899)
12. 'The Ramayana' (Delivered at the Shakespeare Club, Pasadena, California, 31 January 1900)
13. 'The Mahabharata' (Delivered at the Shakespeare Club, Pasadena, California, 1 February 1900)
14. 'Concentration' (Delivered at the Washington Hall, San Francisco, 16 March 1900)
15. 'Meditation' (Delivered at the Washington Hall, San Francisco, 3 April 1900)
16. 'The Practice of Religion' (Delivered at Alameda, California, 18 April 1900)
17. 'Women of India' (Delivered at the Shakespeare Club House, in Pasadena, California, 18 January 1900)
18. 'My Life and Mission' (Delivered at the Shakespeare Club of Pasadena, California, 27 January 1900)
19. 'Buddha's Message to the World' (Delivered in San Francisco, 18 March 1900)
20. 'Is Vedanta the Future Religion?' (Delivered in San Francisco, 8 April 1900)
21. 'Work and its Secret' (Delivered in Los Angeles, California, 4 January 1900)
22. 'The Powers of the Mind' (Delivered in Los Angeles, California, 8 January 1900)

In India

1. 'The Mission of the Vedanta' (Delivered in Kumbakonam, 9 February 1897)
2. 'The Work before Us' (Delivered in Madras, 9 February 1897)
3. 'My Plan of Campaign' (Delivered in Madras, 9 February 1897)
4. 'The Sages of India' (Delivered in Madras, 11 February 1897)
5. 'Vedanta in its Application to Indian Life' (Delivered in Madras, 13 February 1897)
6. 'The Future of India' (Delivered in Madras, 14 February 1897)
7. 'The Vedanta in All Its Phases' (Delivered in Calcutta, 1897)
8. 'The Common Bases of Hinduism' (Delivered in Lahore, 1897)
9. 'Bhakti' (Delivered in Lahore, 9 November 1897)
10. 'The Vedanta' (Delivered in Lahore, 12 November 1897)
11. 'Vedantism' (Delivered in Khetri, Rajasthan, 20 December 1897)
12. 'The Influence of Indian Spiritual Thought in England' (Delivered at Star Theatre, Calcutta, 11 March 1898)
13. 'Sannyasa: Its Ideal and Practice' (Delivered in Belur Math, Calcutta, 19 June 1899)
14. 'What Have I Learnt?' (Delivered in Dacca, 30 March 1901)
15. 'The Religion We Are Born in' (Delivered in Dacca, 31 March 1901)

Glossary

Spiritual and Philosophical Terms

Abhih (fearless): A term often used in spiritual texts to describe a state of fearlessness that comes from self-realization or devotion to the divine.

Anubhav: Experience, particularly in the context of spiritual realization, is valued highly in the Indian philosophical approach.

Atman: The inner self or soul in Hindu philosophy, considered identical to Brahman in Advaita Vedanta.

Bhajans: Devotional songs or hymns sung in praise of the divine.

Bhiksha (alms): The practice of begging for food or sustenance, often done by monks or ascetics as part of their spiritual discipline.

Gerua robe: A saffron-coloured robe worn by Hindu monks and ascetics, symbolizing renunciation and spirituality.

Guru: A spiritual teacher or guide who imparts wisdom and knowledge to their disciples.

Gurubhai: A term used among disciples of the same guru, referring to one another as spiritual brothers.

Guru-Shishya: The traditional relationship between a

guru (teacher) and shishya (disciple), where knowledge is transmitted through direct interaction.

Kamandalu: A water pot carried by Hindu ascetics, symbolizing their renunciation and simple living.

Karma Yogi: A practitioner of Karma Yoga, the path of selfless action and service without attachment to the results.

Mahasamadhi: The conscious and intentional departure from the body by a yogi, regarded as the ultimate liberation.

Mantras and Tantras: Mantras are sacred phrases and sounds chanted in spiritual practices. Tantras refer to texts or practices that involve rituals and meditation.

Nirvikalpa Samadhi: A state of deep meditation where the practitioner experiences non-duality between self and universal energy, directly realizing the ultimate reality.

Nyaya: A school of thought founded by Gautama that focuses on logic and reasoning to seek liberation through valid knowledge.

Parivrajaka Sanyasi: A wandering monk who has renounced worldly life to pursue spiritual enlightenment, often travelling without a fixed abode.

Purva Mimansa: A school of thought founded by Jaimini that focuses on Vedic rituals and duties as a means for maintaining the cosmic order.

Sadhana: Spiritual practice or discipline undertaken to achieve self-realization or spiritual growth.

Samadhi: A state of intense concentration or meditation where the mind becomes completely absorbed in the object of meditation, leading to spiritual enlightenment.

Sanatana Dharma: A set of eternal and universal principles that guide righteous living anchored in Indian spiritual tradition.

Sankhya: A school of thought attributed to Kapila which teaches dualism between consciousness (Purusa) and matter (Prakriti).

Sanyasi: A renunciant who has given up all material possessions and attachments to pursue a life of spiritual discipline.

Shastrartha (intellectual debate): A traditional form of debate on spiritual and philosophical subjects, often involving deep analysis of scriptures.

Shastras: Sacred scriptures or texts in Hinduism, which include the Vedas, Upanishads and other ancient writings that guide religious and philosophical practice.

Shraddha: Faith, devotion, or reverence towards a spiritual path, teacher or deity.

Srimad Bhagavad Gita: A 700-verse Hindu scripture part of the Indian epic Mahabharata, presenting a conversation between prince Arjuna and the god Krishna, which embodies the spiritual foundation of Indian thought, emphasizing duty and self-realization.

Tyag (renunciation) and Seva (service): Key principles in spiritual life, where renunciation refers to the relinquishment of worldly desires, and service denotes selfless acts performed for the benefit of others.

Upanishads: Ancient Indian texts that explore the nature of self (atman) and its unity with the ultimate reality (Brahman).

Uttar Mimansa (Vedanta): A school of thought that focuses on the Upanishadic teachings of atman, Brahman and Moksha (liberation).

Vaisheshika: A school of thought founded by Kanada which enquires in to the nature of reality through the atomic theory.

Vedas: The oldest and the most sacred scriptures of Hinduism, containing hymns, rituals and spiritual wisdom.

Yoga: A system structured by Rishi Patanjali which teaches the union of body, mind and spirit through a step-wise blueprint for attaining the end goal of spiritual liberation.

Cultural and Organizational Terms

Asana: Physical postures in yoga designed to prepare the body and mind for meditation.

Ashtanga Yoga: An eightfold path of yoga described by Patanjali in the *Yoga Sutras*, consisting of Yama, Niyama, Asana, Pranayama, Pratyahara, Dharana, Dhyana and Samadhi.

Ashtavakra Samhita: A classical text on Advaita Vedanta, attributed to the sage Ashtavakra, focusing on non-dualism and self-realization.

Brahmacharis: Individuals who have taken a vow of celibacy and are dedicated to spiritual study and practice.

Dewans: High-ranking officials or ministers in princely states or courts during pre-independence India.

Dharana: The practice of focused concentration on a single point or object, a step in the progression towards meditation.

Dhyana: Meditation, where the mind becomes intensely focused and absorbed in the object of contemplation.

Jnana (knowledge): Spiritual knowledge or wisdom, often associated with self-realization and understanding of the ultimate truth.

Makar Sankranti: A Hindu festival marking the transition of the sun into the zodiac sign of Capricorn, celebrated with various rituals and traditions across India.

Niyama: Personal observances in yoga practice, including purity, contentment and self-discipline.

Paramatman: The Supreme Soul or Universal Self, regarded as the highest reality in Hindu philosophy.

Patanjali: Referring to the sage Patanjali, credited with compiling the *Yoga Sutras*, a foundational text on yoga philosophy.

Prana: The vital life force or energy that flows through all living beings according to Indian philosophy.

Pranayama: Breath control practices in yoga intended to regulate the flow of life force (prana) and enhance concentration.

Pratyahara: The practice of withdrawing the senses from external objects, leading to greater concentration and inner focus.

Raja: A king or monarch in Indian culture, often used to refer to rulers of princely states.

Samadhi: The ultimate state of meditation, where the practitioner experiences unity with the object of meditation and the dissolution of the ego.

Shastra: Another term for scriptures or sacred texts in Hinduism.

Yama: Ethical guidelines or moral imperatives in yoga, including non-violence, truthfulness and self-control.

Bibliography

Abdul Kalam, A.P.J. (Dr), 'Address at The Youth Convention And Inauguration Of The Vivekananda Institute Of Value Education And Culture At Porbandar, Gujarat', 12 January 2006, https://tinyurl.com/5a3pt64c. Accessed on 15 April 2024.

Bhide, Nivedita Raghunath (ed.), *Spiritualizing Life: Book Form of the Talks of Eknathji Ranade*, Vivekananda Kendra Prakashan Trust, Chennai, 2017.

Bhide, Nivedita Raghunath, *On the Mission of Human Evolution: Indian Culture—Challenges & Potentialities*, Vivekananda Kendra Prakashan Trust, Chennai, 2023.

Bhide, Nivedita Raghunath, *Swami Vivekananda in America*, Vivekananda Kendra Prakashan Trust, Chennai, 2002.

Bhuyan, P.R., *Swami Vivekananda: Messiah of Resurgent India*, Atlantic Publishers & Dist., New Delhi, 2003.

Bose, Subhas Chandra, *An Indian Pilgrim: An Unfinished Autobiography*, Sisir Kumar Bose and Sugata Bose (eds.), Oxford University Press, New Delhi, 1997.

Bose, Subhash Chandra, *The Indian Struggle 1920–42*, Sisir Kumar Bose and Sugata Bose (eds.), Oxford University Press, New Delhi, 1997.

DeshGujaratHD, 'APJ Abdul Kalam speaking on Swami

Vivekananda's 150th anniversary function in Gujarat', *YouTube*, 12 January 2012, https://tinyurl.com/4ekrhfcy. Accessed on 15 April 2024.

Dhar, Sailendra Nath, *A Comprehensive Biography of Swami Vivekananda*, Vols 1, 2 and 3, Vivekananda Kendra Prakashan Trust, Chennai, 2012.

Gandhi, M.K., *The Collected works of Mahatma Gandhi* (e-book), Vols 22, 45, 56 and 58, Publications Division Government of India, New Delhi, 1999.

Gandhi, M.K., *The Story of My Experiments with Truth*, Mahadev Desai (trans.), Navajivan Publishing House, Ahmedabad, 1940.

Gupta, Raj Kumar, *The Great Encounter: A Study of Indo-American Literary and Cultural Relations*, Abhinav Publications, New Delhi, 1986.

Indian Institute of Science, https://tinyurl.com/yt8uenx4. Accessed 3 July 2024.

Macaulay, T.B., *Macaulay's Minute on Education*, Central Secretariat Library, Government of India, New Delhi, 1835, https://tinyurl.com/mr3f6hkm. Accessed on 28 July 2025.

Majumdar, R.C. (ed.), *Swami Vivekananda Centenary Memorial Volume*, Swami Vivekananda Centenary, Calcutta, 1963.

Mathai, M.O., *Reminiscences of the Nehru Age*, Vikas Publishing House, New Delhi, 1978.

Modi, Narendra, 'Vivekananda's thoughts have inspired me since childhood', *YouTube*, 6 September 2016, https://tinyurl.com/37zrbhhr. Accessed on 23 February 2024.

Narendra Modi, 'Glimpses of Day 1 of Vivekananda Yuva Vikas Yatra', 12 September 2012, https://tinyurl.com/295yzvd8. Accessed on 26 July 2024.

Narendra Modi, 'India is changing. India's standing at the global stage is rising and this is due to Jan Shakti: PM', 11 September 2017, https://tinyurl.com/23nc7ytx. Accessed on 23 February 2024.

Narendra Modi, 'PM Modi and President Obama Share their Thoughts Together on Mann ki Baat', 27 January 2015, https://tinyurl.com/ybapntjt. Accessed on 18 June 2024.

Narendra Modi, 'Tough Line on Black Money: Full Text of PM Modi's Interview To Network 18', 2 September 2016, https://tinyurl.com/234f2fz9. Accessed on 23 February 2024.

NDTV, '"Feel A Divine Energy": PM Modi's Note After Meditating At Vivekananda Rock Memorial,' 1 June 2024. https://tinyurl.com/2uskx5t5. Accessed on 18 June 2024.

Nehru, Jawaharlal, *Glimpses of World History, 18th impression*, Jawaharlal Nehru Memorial Fund and Oxford University Press, New Delhi, 2003.

Nehru, Jawaharlal, *The Discovery of India*, Oxford University Press, New Delhi, 1989. First published 1946.

Pravrajika Atmaprana, *Sister Nivedita*, Sister Nivedita Girls' School, Calcutta, 2017. First Published 1961.

Pravrajika Atmaprana, *Western Women in the Footsteps of Swami Vivekananda*, Ramakrishna Sarada Mission, Hauz Khas, New Delhi, 1995.

Pravrajika Vrajaprana, *My Faithful Goodwin*, Advaita Ashrama, Uttarakhand, 2015. First Published 1994.

Press Information Bureau, 'PM's address at the Closing Ceremony of the Commemoration of 150th Birth Anniversary of Swami Vivekananda', 12 January 2014 https://tinyurl.com/2f8x3yfx. Accessed on 26 July 2023.

Press Information Bureau, 'Prime Minister Shri Narendra Modi unveils statue of Swami Vivekananda at JNU Campus', 6 October 2022, https://tinyurl.com/yttyhatm. Accessed on 24 October 2024.

Rahbar, Hansraj, *Vivekananda: The Warrior Saint*, 10th Ed., Vijay Goel English-Hindi Publisher, Delhi, 2009.

Ramakrishna Math and Mission, 'About Us', https://donations.belurmath.org/about-us. Accessed on 29 March 2022.

Ramakrishna Mission Institute of Culture, *History of Science in India: An Introduction*, Kolkata, 2015.

Ramakrishna Mission Institute of Culture, *Nivedita of India*, Kolkata, 2016. First published 2002.

Ranade, Eknath, *The Story of The Vivekananda Rock Memorial*, Vivekananda Kendra Prakashan Trust, Chennai, 2017.

Rolland, Romain, *The Life of Ramakrishna*, Advaita Ashrama, Uttarakhand, 2023. First Published 1929.

Rolland, Romain, *The Life of Vivekananda and the Universal Gospel*, Advaita Ashrama, Uttarakhand, 2018. First Published 1931.

Roy, Samaren, *M.N. Roy: A Political Biography*, Orient Longman, New Delhi, 1997.

Roy, Shubhajit, 'George Bush, Barack Obama, Donald Trump:

Reading American Presidents India visit', *The Indian Express*, 28 February 2020, https://tinyurl.com/29srd2wj. Accessed on 7 August 2024.

Sanborn, Kate, *Abandoning An Adopted Farm*, D. Appleton and Company, New York, 1906.

Shri Golwalkar Guruji, 'Glimpses of a Great Soul', https://tinyurl.com/38rzewt5. Accessed on 30 June 2022.

Sister Nivedita, *The Master as I Saw Him*, 9th ed., Kolkata: Udbodhan Office, 1962, 36th reprint, 2016.

Swami Ghanananda and Geoffrey Parrinder, *Swami Vivekananda in East and West*, Ramakrishna Vedanta Centre, London, 1968.

Swami Nikhileswarananda, 'Lecture of Abdul Kalam on Birthday of Swami Vivekananda', *YouTube*, 5 June 2020, https://tinyurl.com/mt2c8nt6. Accessed on 15 April 2024.

Swami Ranganathananda, *Universal Message of the Bhagavad Gita Vol. 1*, Advaita Ashrama, Uttarakhand, 2000.

Swami Ranganathananda, *Universal Message of the Bhagavad Gita Vol. 2*, Advaita Ashrama, Uttarakhand, 2000.

Swami Vivekananda, 'Collegiate Days—Tendencies,' https://tinyurl.com/ytmftakh. Accessed on 2 May 2025.

Swami Vivekananda, *Chicago Addresses*, Advaita Ashrama, Uttarakhand, 2018. First Published 1993.

Swami Vivekananda, *My India: The India Eternal*, (1st ed.), Ramakrishna Mission Institute of Culture, Kolkata, 1993, 24th Reprint 2019.

Swami Vivekananda, *Raja Yoga: Or Conquering the Internal*

Nature, Advaita Ashrama, Uttarakhand, 3rd Edition, 2017. 8th reprint, 2023.

Swami Vivekananda, *The Complete Works of Swami Vivekananda* (Vols I, II, III, IV, V, VI, VII, VIII, IX), Advaita Ashrama, Uttarakhand, 2016.

TATA, 'A Meeting On Board the Empress of India', https://tinyurl.com/s4x2r9fm. Accessed on 16 December 2023.

Tesla Memorial Society of New York, 'Nikola Tesla and Swami Vivekananda', n.d., https://tinyurl.com/57zxcc9n. Accessed on 24 August 2023.

The Gospel of Sri Ramakrishna (Red Letter Ed.), Originally recorded in Bengali by M., a disciple of Sri Ramakrishna; Sri Ramakrishna Math Mylapore, Chennai, 1942, (Red Letter Ed. 2000).

The Harvard Crimson, 'Vivekananda's Address', 17 May 1894, https://tinyurl.com/2k9583ku. Accessed on 7 August 2024.

The Life of Swami Vivekananda by His Eastern and Western Disciples, Vols 1 and 2, Advaita Ashrama, Uttarakhand, 6th Edition, 1989. 19th reprint, 2023.

The White House, 'Remarks by President Obama in Address to the People of India', 27 January 2015, https://tinyurl.com/48nwp332. Accessed on 7 August 2024.

Vivekananda Rock Memorial & Vivekananda Kendra, 'Vivekananda Kendra—Spiritually Oriented Service Mission, https://tinyurl.com/3wjhetcn. Accessed on 23 February 2024.

Index

Abdul Kalam, A.P.J., 82, 83
Advaita, ix, 18, 40, 138, 141
Akasha, 49, 50
Almora, 14, 35, 71
Alwar, xii, 15
Ambedkar, B.R., 73
Annadurai, C.N., 88
anubhav, 68
atman, 47, 140, 141
Ayodhya, 14, 17

Bangalore/Bengaluru, xii, 16
Baranagar Math, 14
Basham, A.L., xviii
Basu, Jyoti, 89, 90
Basu, Kamala, 90
Belur Math, 4, 14, 39, 40, 43, 75, 86, 105
bhiksha, 16
Biley, 4
Bose, Jagadish Chandra, 40

Bose, Subhas Chandra (see also, Netaji), 70
brahmacharya, 34
Brahman, 50, 138, 140, 141
Brahmâvadin, 35
Brahmo Samaj, 2, 6, 9, 10, 75
British East India Company, 1
British India, 2
British Raj, 2
Buddha, 53, 73, 74
Buddhism, 29, 74, 109

Calcutta/Kolkata, xi, xii, xiii, 2, 3, 4, 5, 6, 11, 42, 75, 103, 137
California, 40
Chakravarti, Renu, 88
Chicago, xvii, 3, 16, 18, 19, 20, 21, 22, 25, 31, 32, 81, 85, 86, 120

Chicago World's Fair, 22
Congress of the History of Religions, 40

Dakshineshwar Temple, xvii, 105, 106
Datta, Vishwanath, 4, 8
Devi, Bhuvaneshwari, 4
Devi, Sarada, 9, 71, 108
divine, ix, xiii, xix, 9, 17, 47, 52, 53, 54, 56, 64, 65, 73, 86, 110, 111, 112, 138

First Arts Examination, 6

Ganga, 5, 6
Goodwin, J.J., xi, 33, 34, 36, 38
gurubhai, 19, 31, 33, 37, 40
guru-shishya, 12

Hastie, William, 7, 9
Holy Mother, 9, 71

Indian Institute of Science, xii, 81
India's first war of independence, 2
International Congress of Physics, 40
Ishvara, 49, 50

Junagarh, 15

Kalyanasundaram, Meenakshisundaram, 89
kamandalu, 14, 18
Kamarpukur, 9
Kanyakumari, 16, 18, 20, 38, 80, 86, 87, 132
Khetri, xii, 15, 20, 37

Lahore, xi, 3, 35
Lohia, Ram Manohar, 88
Los Angeles, 40

Macaulay, 1
MacLeod, Josephine, 34
Madras, xi, xii, 16, 35, 38, 89, 137
mahasamadhi, xii, 43, 139
Mahat, 49, 50
Mahatma Gandhi, 74
Mathai, M.O., 73
Minute on Education, 1, 2
Modi, Narendra, 84
Müller, Max, 21, 24, 35, 36

Narendranath, 4, 5, 6, 7, 8, 9, 10, 11, 13, 14
Netaji, 70, 71, 72
New York, 31, 32, 33, 40, 49, 135
nirvikalpa samadhi, 9

Obama, Barack, 86

Pandurang, Pandit Shankar, 15, 16
paramatman, 47
Paramhansa, Ramakrishna, xi, xii, xv, xvii, 3, 6, 9, 10, 11, 12, 13, 14, 31, 35, 36, 37, 39, 42, 44, 70, 71, 72, 75, 76, 77, 79, 103, 105, 106, 108
Paris, 40
parivrajaka sanyasi, 14
Pasadena, 40, 136
Patanjali, 30, 53, 141, 142
Patanjali's *Yoga Sutras*, 30
Perumal, Maharaja Alasinga, 20, 25
Porbandar, 82
Prabuddha Bharata, xii
practical spirituality, vii, 90

Practical Vedanta, 50, 51, 133
Prana, 30, 49, 50, 142
Presidency College, 6
Puri, Tota, 9

Radhakrishnan, Sarvepalli, xiii, 80
Rahbar, Hansraj, 78
Raipur, 5
Raja Yoga, viii, 21, 30, 75
Ramakrishna Mission, xi, xii, 39, 41, 71, 75, 76, 79, 103
Ramayana, 17, 136
Rameswaram Temple, 61
Ranade, Eknathji, 79, 87, 91, 97
Rockefeller, John D., 21, 32, 33
Rolland, Romain, xiv, xv, xvi, 12, 20, 29, 31

sadhana, 9
Sanborn, Kate, 24, 25
San Francisco, 23, 40, 136
Scottish Church College, 6, 7
Sen, Keshub Chandra, 35

seva, 13, 116, 122
shastrartha, 68
Shastri, Lal Bahadur, 88
shraddha, 12, 55
Singh, Maharaja Ajit, 15, 20, 21, 31
Singh, Raghunath, 88
Sister Christine, 36
Sister Gargi, xv
Sister Nivedita, xi, xii, xv, 36, 40, 41, 42, 44, 69, 74, 105, 106, 108, 147, 148
social justice, 73
Srimad Bhagavad Gita, 14, 52, 65, 140
Swami Abhedananda, 31
Swami Akhandananda, xii, 37, 79
Swami Ramakrishnananda, xii, 19, 35
Swami Turiyananda, 40

Tagore, Devendranath, 10
Tagore, Rabindranath, xv, 12, 79
Tesla, Nikola, 49, 50
The Nineteenth Century, 36
Tilak, Bal Gangadhar, xv, 18, 80

tyag, 13, 116, 122

Udaipur, xii
Udbodhan, xii
Upanishad, 42, 46, 47, 48, 58, 65, 102, 132, 140

Vajpayee, Atal Bihari, 88
Vandemata, 5
Varanasi, 16, 17, 40, 43
Vedanta, v, viii, xi, xiii, xvii, 3, 13, 18, 20, 21, 29, 31, 34, 36, 38, 46, 47, 48, 50, 51, 52, 53, 56, 59, 60, 65, 67, 68, 78, 92, 109, 111, 112, 132, 133, 136, 137, 138, 141
Vedanta Societies, xi, 21
Vedanta Society of New York, 31
Vedantists, 46
Vidyasagar, Pt. Ishwar Chandra, 5
Vrindavan, 14, 17

Wimbledon, 40
World Parliament of Religions, xvii, 3, 18, 20, 21, 22, 25, 28, 74, 75, 112